Carl i...

Orville Johnson was the
son of Mrs. Johnson of
Summers, Ark. a very
faithful member of First
Bapt. Church of Summers
Ark when I was pastor
there 1959-1961. Orville

Never Touch a Tiger

& his Wife Mary are Bible
translators for Wycliff.

Never Touch
a
Tiger

by Hugh Steven

THOMAS NELSON PUBLISHERS
Nashville

Unless otherwise noted, Scripture verses used in this book are from the King James Version.

Verses marked TLB are taken from *The Living Bible* (Wheaton, Ill.: Tyndale House Publishers, 1971) and are used by permission.

Library of Congress Cataloging in Publication Data

Steven, Hugh.
   Never touch a tiger.

   1. Johnson, Mary, 1927-   2. Secoya Indians—Missions.   3. Indians of Mexico—Missions. 4. Missionaries—Mexico—Biography. 5. Missionaries—Ecuador—Biography. 6. Wycliffe Bible Translators. 7. Indians of South America—Ecuador—Missions.
I. Title.
F3722.1.S43J637   266'.0092'4 [B]   80-18225
ISBN 0-8407-5737-9

Dedicated to Orville and Mary
and to their children
Omar
Roger
David
Ginger

Table of Contents

Acknowledgments

As in every writing assignment, more information is gathered than is used in the story. This necessitates asking a great deal of questions—sometimes, I'm sure, to the chagrin of the ones being interviewed. Thank you to all who patiently and graciously offered stories, memories, and insights about Mary and Orv—people like Wilbur and Evelyn Aulie; Marianna Slocum; Gladys Woods; Lois Peterson; Bill Anders; Roy Gleason; Bub and Bobbie Borman, and their son Randy; and two of Mary and Orv's children, Ginger and David.

There were others who helped me, but time and space preclude a lengthy recital of names. However, I want to say a special word of appreciation to Mary's mother, Elodia; to Orv; and to Mary herself, who was most patient and accommodating to my probing. I also want to thank Don and Helen Johnson for their love and gracious hospitality, and for the hospitality of Wycliffe's Ecuador branch.

A special thanks goes to my secretary, Jocelyn Cameron, for her enthusiasm and endless hours of typing, and to my wife, Norma, who remains my constant helper, supporter, and efficient editor.

Introduction

This is first of all the story of a woman named Mary—a woman who is almost never bored, who has experienced physical and emotional isolation, who loves others deeply, who has a great host of friends yet experiences profound moments of loneliness. It is about a woman who is competent, caring, and who always comes through in the crunch, yet who bears dark, nagging fears that she is unqualified to carry out the tasks assigned to her by God and man.

The goal of some books is to tell about a person's life. That is important and valuable. But in this book I want the readers to see and feel more than the people and events in Mary's life. I desire that readers find for themselves an answer to the question, "Of what is one's life?"

A great many philosophers have attempted to answer this question. I feel the apostle Paul provides the most satisfying of answers: "For to me to live is Christ, and to die is gain" (Phil. 1:21). Jim Conway, writing in HIS magazine, once wrote, "The purpose of Paul's life was not to guarantee his rights, his pleasures, his health or his happiness, but his purpose was to serve God and other people."

This book is about this kind of person.

Hugh Steven
Santa Ana, California

CHAPTER ONE

The Adventurer

The birthday party was grand. A band of local Mexican musicians had exhausted themselves and the partygoers with polkas, *pasa dobles,* quadrilles, reels, schottisches, and waltzes. As he had done several times before at such parties, six-foot-four-inch Stanford Morison asked Judith Trejo for the first dance.

Dressed in a high-collared, floor-length, white cotton dress, Judith extended her hand. Her sleeves were long and tied tight at the wrists with lace ruffles like the one around her neck. Her boots were black and buttoned up to her shapely mid-calf. Her long dress covered her boots and ruffled petticoat, and with the first strains of the music, Stanford placed his strong hand around her waist, and together they began to skip and twirl and otherwise frolic around the wooden storehouse floor.

"You are the best dancer and the most important person in Tumbalá," said Judith. "Why do you always ask me to dance first?"

"Because I like you and want to marry you," replied Stanford, as they walked toward an empty bench after finishing their dance.

Judith sat down and quizzically eyed the tall American.

"Ah! You mock me!" she said.

"No, it's true. I have watched you ever since you came to Tumbalá. I like you, and I truly want to marry you."

"How can you say such words to me? I am the poorest person in Tumbalá. And you, with all your coffee plantations, must be the richest. Also you have an education, and I have had only three months in school. I am not in your class. I'm just a poor Mexican girl. I can offer you nothing."

"You have a quick mind, and I think you are the prettiest girl in town," countered Stanford. "Whether you are rich or poor isn't important to me. I like people for what they are, and I like you. I want to marry you!"

"I don't believe you! I can't believe you!" Judith retorted angrily. "You shouldn't talk to me like this. Here we have come for a party, and you talk of serious things and make fun of me. You are like all rich people— always taking advantage of poor people. Why do you want to take advantage of a poor girl like me?"

The year was 1894. Rather than heeding Horace Greeley's words to "Go west, young man," twenty-five-year-old Stanford Newell Morison had come south to the state of Chiapas in Old Mexico.

And why not? Stanford's world—particularly his

home town of St. Paul, Minnesota, was awash with the drama and excitement of the previous eighty years.

Sometimes known as the Little Boston of the West, St. Paul in the 1800s provided a front-row balcony seat to a string of stirring cultural, industrial, and historical dramas: The Louisiana Purchase; the official opening of large tracts of land west of the Mississippi to throngs of settlers; Indian treaties; and the last major Sioux attempt to drive out the white man from the Indians' hunting grounds. There was also statehood; the Civil War; the Mayo clinic; and a new railroad that propelled settlers and visitors across the plains at the staggering speed of fifty-five miles per hour.

It was in fact this railroad, or more correctly James R. Hill, the developer of the Great Northern Railroad, who greatly influenced Stanford Morison. By the late 1800s the burly Hill was a well-known businessman who had earned the name "Empire Builder" for developing the area between the Great Lakes and the Pacific Northwest. He was also Stanford Morison's neighbor and a close family friend.

Others had influenced Stanford too, like Yale's football coach and athletic director Walter Chauncy Camp. Often called the "father of American football," Camp published a series of simple physical exercises, now known as the daily dozen. His other publications contributed greatly to clean play and sportsmanship.

But it never bothered Camp's keen sense of fair play to use the sturdy six-foot-four, 240-pound Morison as right guard. In 1891, Walter Camp's Yale football team was invincible!

And invincible describes how Stanford Morison felt when he graduated from Yale in pre-med. He had experienced success on the gridiron. All his models were successful. Even his uncle and namesake, Stanford Newell Morison, was the U.S. ambassador to the Netherlands.

The whole world seemed to be standing on tiptoe, waiting for yet another new marvel. Men were trying to fly through the air on motorized airplanes. There was a machine called a Gramophone that you could wind up to play music. An instrument they called the telephone carried your voice to another person miles away.

Then there was that marvelous invention, the Stanley Steamer. This snorting monster soon gave way to the more sophisticated and "safer" gasoline-powered automobile. Oh, what an age to be alive!

Amid this high mood of adventure and with a recent family inheritance, Stanford and his two brothers each set out to find their own adventure. To the surprise of his family and many of his aristocratic friends, Stanford didn't choose to become a physician or to invest in the cutting edge of U.S. industry. Rather, he chose to represent the German-American coffee interests in Chiapas, Mexico.

For two days the women of Tumbalá, in the state of Chiapas, had spent long, back-breaking hours hand-grinding precooked corn kernels into *masa* (dough) to make the huge quantities of tortillas required for Stanford Morison's birthday party. And since it was *Dõn* Stanford's fortieth birthday, the village spared no expense.

Actually, the manager of Stanford's, or the Morison Company General Store, was the instigator of this party and all others involving a general invitation to the villagers. Stanford loved to dance and was without doubt the best dancer for a hundred miles around. The manager knew this, and he took every opportunity to clear out the big storehouse and convert it into a dance floor.

The manager used Stanford's food and money for the party. A steer was cut up and boiled in large clay casseroles. But if Stanford knew, he didn't care. It was his policy to start a business, put someone in charge, go off on a business trip, and forget about it. He didn't care because he could afford it. In less than ten years Stanford (his brothers didn't take to rural Mexican life and left shortly after their arrival) had become the owner-operator of the *Esperanza,* a huge coffee plantation. Before five more years passed, he owned two more—the *Alianza* and *Agua Azul.*

In 1903, Tumbalá was almost like it is today—a gloomy village with narrow, rutted, cobblestone streets filled with the constant clatter of mule trains coming and going. Alongside each narrow street are single-story board houses with dull, rust-colored, tile roofs. Many seem to function as a combination store and living quarters—not a store like the big stores in Tuxtla, but one with a few shelves of assorted candles, cheap candies, flour, salt, unrefined sugar, and a few tins of sardines. Those that don't sell cheap candy and assorted foodstuffs sell liquor—most of it volatile.

But the main reason for Tumbalá's gloominess is the rain and fog. For ten months of the year, heavy clouds from the plains of Tabasco back up against the 4,900-foot-high mountain village and dump their depressing cargo of drizzle, rain, and fog.

In 1903, a forty-minute walk to the north and down the mountain slope to an elevation of 4,300 feet brought you to a warm, sunny plain overlooking the Gulf of

Mexico. Heavily forested with tall Ponderosa pines, it seemed to Stanford an ideal spot for his coffee plantations. He chose the *Alianza* to build his coffee-processing sheds and house.

With kiln-dried lumber, Stanford constructed the largest frame house anyone in Tumbalá had ever seen. It was painted blue, had seven rooms, a galvanized metal roof, and a veranda that girdled the entire structure. The Chol Indians who worked the coffee plantation were sure there was enough room on the veranda alone to accommodate more than a dozen Chol families. And the Indians were amazed to find that Stanford lived in it by himself—without a wife!

But Stanford was about to change that. He was firmly established as one of the most influential and popular coffee ranchers in the area, and he had begun to look more selectively at the black-eyed *señoritas* who came to his parties. On the night of his birthday party, he made his selection.

Her name was Judith. She was sixteen and pretty, with a small, energetic figure and bright black eyes. When she smiled, cute little mischievous dimples formed at the edges of her mouth.

She was also from one of the poorest families in town. Her father, a kindly man, had been a public scribe, carpenter, and tailor in the lowland town of Chilón, an eight-hour walk from Tumbalá. But like too many men before and after him, he eventually drank himself and his family into poverty. His death was no surprise, and he left Judith, her mother, and two sisters destitute. There had been another brother and sister, but this family had suffered the all-too-common anguish of watching children die before their time.

In her desperation, Judith's mother turned for help

and support to a dowager aunt who lived in Tumbalá. A severe woman, the aunt agreed to help, then chided Judith's mother and the children bitterly for getting themselves into such a mess.

Several days after the gala party, Stanford, riding on his mule, spotted Judith, also on a mule. Both were on their way to Judith's eldest sister's wedding. Stanford had been asked to be the *padrino* (a special friend who provides the wedding feast). The selection of the *padrino* usually falls to the godparents. In this case there were no godparents, but there was Stanford. And since he was one of the wealthiest of the two thousand people around Tumbalá, and since a wedding meant a three-day celebration of feasting, drinking, and dancing, Stanford was happy to be chosen.

"Muy buenos días, Lolita," said Stanford, grinning.

"How do you know my nickname?" asked Judith with mocked indignation.

"I know a great many things," he answered.

"And I know lots of things, too."

"What things do you know?"

"Things like, you are going back to your home in the United States."

"Just partly true," he replied, adjusting himself in the saddle. "It is true I am going to the United States. But I am going on a business trip, not to live. And this is why I must speak to you. There is a girl back in the States. She made me promise a year ago that I would come back in a year's time. I'm going back to fulfill that promise, but I don't want to marry her. I want you to promise not to marry anyone while I'm gone, because when I come back, I want to marry you."

19

Believing he was still teasing her, Judith broke her mule into a canter with a quick slap of the reins.

"Wait!" called Stanford, digging his spurs hard into his mule's flanks. "You haven't given me your promise. Have you promised someone else?"

"Oh no," laughed Judith. "That is too dangerous."

"What do you mean?" he asked.

"When I was fifteen," she explained, "I loved a man who was about twenty-two. We used to write letters and talk of love and how wonderful it would be to be married and away from my aunt who made me work hard sewing dresses."

"That doesn't sound too dangerous to me," said Stanford with a wry smile.

"Oh, but I am not finished. It made me happy for someone to give me such attention. But one day at a fiesta dance I discovered he had another girl friend, and I was angry. When I got home, I wrote a letter to tell him I never wanted to see him again."

"What happened then?" asked Stanford. He was enjoying this opportunity to learn more about the girl he intended to make his bride.

"Several days later, I was sitting on my aunt's veranda sewing when he rode up. I could tell by the way his horse galloped he was angry. He stopped his horse with a hard jerk of the reins right in front of me.

" 'Is it true as you said in your letter that you never want to see me again?' he demanded.

"I was frightened, but I kept on sewing, pretending not to be upset. I told him I wouldn't have said it if I didn't mean it, and I didn't want any husband who had another girl friend!

"All this time I had been looking down at my sewing.

When I told him I wouldn't marry him, I looked up into his eyes. They were ablaze with furious anger. When he saw I was serious about what I said, he spun his horse around, drew his pistol, turned in his saddle, and shouted, 'If you won't marry me, then I will kill you before anyone else does.' Then he fired his pistol at me and galloped off!"

"How terrible for you!" Stanford sympathized.

"It would have been, if he had hit me. But he didn't shoot straight, and the bullet made a hole in the sombrero of a Chol Indian man who was also sitting on the veranda!"

Judith and Stanford laughed together as she described the look of comical shock on the poor man's face. As they approached the church, Stanford again reminded Judith of his intention to return and marry her.

"I haven't promised anybody anything," she said with a laugh. "And when you return, I expect you will find me just as you see me now."

Stanford was a man committed to being true to himself and to his word, and he returned to Tumbalá as he had promised. Also as he had promised, he again asked Judith to marry him. As before, Judith could not believe he was serious.

"Here we are at this first dance in honor of your return," she said, "and as before you mock me with talk of marriage."

"You don't understand," said Stanford. "I am not making fun of you. I want to marry you."

"If your words are true," she countered, "then you

21

must ask me in the right way—not at a party like this. If you have serious things to talk about, you must first talk to my mother."

"I don't understand," said Stanford. "I see all the other fellows talking to their girls like this. How is it that you are so particular?"

In every culture there is an order of things, a proper pattern for interpersonal conduct before relationships are established and built. However, under special circumstances such rites are overlooked, especially if it is profitable to do so.

In Judith's case, the advantage resulting from marrying Stanford would be enormous. As the daughter of a poor widow, she knew that no matter how much she wanted her life to be different, she was probably forever locked into her class as a servant. Marriage, which was inevitable, would only provide a new set of problems for her.

Yet knowing this was her chance of a lifetime, Judith said, "I am not like other girls. It may be all right for them, but it is not all right for me." There was in that declaration the strength of a simple dignity that insisted on upholding her sense of order, even when she was offered an unbelievable new lifestyle. And because Stanford was the gentleman he was, he saw that dignity and respected Judith's wishes.

Overjoyed with the prospect of a tall American for a son-in-law, Judith's mother gave her blessing. "It would be good for you if he wants to marry you." But her aunt accused Stanford of duplicity. One day Judith overheard her aunt say to Stanford, "Surely you are not going to marry Lolita. I have heard that your friends are aghast at the thought of your marrying the poorest girl in town. Haven't they suggested the names of some young girls from Mexican society?"

"It is true that my business friends have suggested that I marry into what they consider to be 'proper society,' but I am in love with Judith."

"That is a lie! All you want from Lolita is what you can get from her."

"No! What you say is false. I love Judith and I am truly going to marry her and love her till the day I die."

"Ha! Words. If what you say is true, why hasn't she said yes? It has been almost a year since you asked her mother for permission."

"Judith is young," said Stanford. "She's only seventeen, and she has needed all this time to convince herself I am serious and that I am not going to go back to the United States without her. Furthermore," he added, "I have just come from visiting her mother and grandmother, and we have set the date."

"You mean she said she would marry you?"

"Yes," said Stanford. "We are to be married immediately!"

By 1821, Mexico had just thrown off three centuries of Spanish rule and had gone through a deeply complex series of revolts and governmental changes. Prior to 1821 and the Plan of Iguala (which proclaimed Mexico to be a constitutional monarchy), no Mexican had ever held office in local government, voted in an election, or debated in Parliament. All this had been the prerogative of the Spanish viceroys.

Between 1821 and 1894, the year Stanford Morison first crossed the Rio Grande, Mexico had experienced political unrest, civil war, and the devastating loss of some of its territories. Then came 1876, and Porfírio Díaz assumed the presidency. For the next thirty years, Díaz ruled Mexico with a firm, often ruthless authoritarianism.

By the turn of the century, it was safe for foreigners to travel on most Mexican highways without fear of attack or banditry. With his open-door policy of foreign capital investment, Díaz saw his country's railroad mileage increase from 430 to 15,000. Foreign trade multiplied ten times, the petroleum industry was started, and Stanford Morrison had his three large coffee plantations.

But like many other dictators, Díaz's insensitivity to the needs of the masses, plus the wholesale distribution of Mexican natural resources to foreign entrepreneurs, fomented the revolution of 1910. From the southern state of Morelia came Emiliano Zapata, and from the northern state of Chihuahua came controversial Pancho Villa. Both men backed the man they felt would change the Díaz dictatorship—the five-foot-two-inch man with a high-pitched voice and a brown beard—Francisco Madero.

Three years later, Madero was imprisoned and ultimately assassinated, leaving the country in the hands of General Victoriano Huerta. Believing that Mexico was seething with discontent, many Americans returned to the United States. But Stanford Morison was not among them, at least not then. He had fallen in love with Mexico and with one of its most beautiful young women. Stanford believed he had chosen Mexico's finest, and he didn't want a pesky revolution hundreds of miles away to interfere.

24

Shortly after their marriage in 1910, Stanford asked his young wife if she had ever read the Apocrypha.

"I have never even heard this strange word. What is it?" she asked.

"It's part of the Catholic Bible," he answered. "There's a story in it about a crafty woman named Judith."

"Tell me about it," she said excitedly.

"Judith was a beautiful young widow who decided to do something about her besieged city. One night she put on perfume, dressed in her finest clothes, and lied her way into the tent of the commanding general of the enemy armies. She told the guards she could tell them how to get into her city.

"When the commander-in-chief saw this beautiful woman, he had a great desire for her. Cleverly, as only you women can do, Judith led him on and got him drunk. When the commander-in-chief could no longer stand, Judith siezed the opportunity, grabbed his sword, and with two quick blows cut off his head."

"Oh, how terrible!" said Judith.

"It did the job," said Stanford, "just like David did on Goliath. When the enemy army realized their commander-in-chief had been killed, they all fled, and Judith led her people in a great thanksgiving feast. I've always thought that was a grisly story, so my darling Lolita, from now on I am going to call you Elodia." And from that moment on she was forever Elodia.

Between 1910 (the Morisons' wedding year) and 1914, the Morison company flourished—especially the *Alianza*—revolutionary activity notwithstanding. Mule trains were constantly taking coffee out and bringing trade goods in. And Elodia found her own level as a hard-working wife and gracious hostess to the many guests, visitors, and those who needed a night's lodging.

But the years were bittersweet. Their first child, Harry, died at age three from pneumonia. It would be ten years before there were more children; meanwhile, Stanford and Elodia become unwilling actors in the high drama of the Mexican Revolution.

CHAPTER TWO

Clean Clothes Are Washed Without Soap

Elodia heard them first—the clink, clink of silver spurs and the occasional pawing of a nervous horse. She slipped out of bed and heard another sound—three resonant gongs from the ornate grandfather clock that had been a gift from the members of Stanford's Yale football team. Silently Elodia tiptoed to the window, pulled back the curtain, and peeked out.

The moon was full, and in the pale light she saw a large circle of uniformed horsemen. Elodia couldn't make out the color of the uniforms, but she saw that most of the men wore broad felt hats. The uniforms seemed to be gray, with red ties and silver buttons—the *Rurales*.

The *Rurales*, or rural policemen, were holdovers from the days of Porfírio Díaz. Now these same men could be *Federales* under Huerta, or Constitutionalists loyal to

Pancho Villa and the new man who was to be the provisional president, Venustiano Carranza. Or they could be *guerrilleros*—guerrillas.

Quietly, Elodia slipped back to the bed and shook Stanford's shoulder. "There are soldiers outside," she whispered. "They have surrounded the house. I don't know what it means."

"Well, I'll find out right now." Stanford pulled on his pants and slipped into his shoes.

His tall, broad-shouldered frame almost filled the doorway as he asked the waiting horsemen, "What is it that you want?"

"We want you!" came the curt reply from a mustachioed officer. "And right now!"

"But why?" asked Stanford.

"You'll find out soon enough. We have orders to take you to Ocosingo."

"All right, I'll come with you as soon as I get something to eat. In the meantime, why don't you come in out of the cool night air? My wife will make some coffee."

Outwardly calm but inwardly tormented at the drama occurring before her eyes, Elodia made a fire in the cast iron stove and heated water for coffee. She was used to serving large groups of people, but these thirty sullen, unshaven men upset her. It wasn't just that they had come to take away her husband; she also was bothered by the way they looked and nodded to each other when she walked by. Yet she served each man as if he were an invited guest.

But welcome guests they were not, and when they left with Stanford they cut what they thought were the *Alianza* telephone lines. They actually cut the lines of a rival German rancher known for his brutal treatment of his Chol Indian workers.

Immediately after Stanford was taken, the foreman of the *Alianza* telephoned the other two ranches, and they in turn made plans to contact the American embassy in Mexico City. Unaware that all this was taking place, Elodia began her own strategy. She spoke to the town secretary.

"I am truly sorry to hear of *Don* Stanford's misfortune," said the secretary. "But what can I do?"

"You can write a letter to the authorities and tell them Stanford has no interest in politics. You can tell them Stanford is a man who loves Mexico and the people of Tumbalá."

"Oh *Señora,* you do not know what you are asking me to do. These are hard times. I don't want to speak against the government."

"I am not asking you to speak against the government," said Elodia. "I only ask that you speak for Stanford's character."

"Believe me, I would truly like to help you, but to do even that would be politically unwise for me."

Stanford had been right to credit Elodia with a quick mind. It was also a mind that remained calm under pressure.

"Did you think it was politically unwise for you when you asked Stanford to be the *padrino* at your daughter's wedding?" asked Elodia with arched eyebrows. "And when your wife was sick and Stanford loaned you money to take her to the hospital in Tuxtla, was that also politically unwise? I suppose it was, since you have not yet returned the loan!"

"*Señora,* your tongue is sharp and painful. *Don* Stanford did help me when I needed help, yet there is still no way I can help you without getting myself into trouble."

Elodia next asked the town scribe to publish an article on Stanford's behalf.

"You know Stanford is a just man," pleaded Elodia. "He has no interest in politics. He doesn't cheat his workers. He pays them fairly and doesn't mistreat them."

"What you say is no doubt true," said the man. "But times are bad. It would be madness for me to publish an article telling what a fine man *Don* Stanford is. It would appear I was contradicting government action. I know you are in pain, *Señora*. All of us are these days. Perhaps if you remember the old proverb it would help."

"Proverb?" asked Elodia. "What old proverb?"

"*Ropa blanca se lava sin jabón* (Clean clothes are washed without soap)," quoted the scribe.

Never for a moment did Elodia doubt Stanford's innocence. Fervently she tried to rally his trusted employees to speak up for him. None would. Unashamedly, they admitted their fear. But there was another reason, one that momentarily gripped Elodia's stomach with her own kind of fear.

"We have heard, *Señora*," they said, "that the soldiers have shot and killed *Don* Stanford."

"Do you know this for sure?" asked Elodia.

"Not for sure," they said, "but it is what everyone in Tumbalá is saying."

With no one to offer her support or encouragement, Elodia returned to her mother's house in Tumbalá. Within a few short hours, Elodia's happy, carefree life had crashed in around her. And from the thin smiles on the faces of some of her friends, it seemed they were almost glad about this misfortune. Elodia was confronting a universal paradox: Society is often as pitiless to those who succeed as it is to those who fail.

"I do not know if the rumor is true or not," said Elodia to her mother. "Therefore, I must find out for myself."

"How will you do this?" asked her mother.

"I am going to Ocosingo."

"Ocosingo! *Ay*, Daughter, you will be attacked on the trail. Can't some of the workers from the *Alianza* go for you?"

"I have asked them. They are all afraid. And I am not going to sit here in this cold, rainy town with my arms folded, waiting and listening to rumors that my husband is dead." As Elodia made preparations to leave, she heard someone calling her name.

"*Señora* Morison, *Señora* Morison!"

"It's the lame one, Francisco Lopez, from the *Esperanza*," said Elodia to her mother as she opened the door to welcome him.

"*Señora* Morison," said Francisco, "I heard you are planning to go yourself to Ocosingo to find *Don* Stanford."

"It is true," said Elodia. "No one in Tumbalá will go for me."

"It is dangerous for a young woman to be on the trail in these times," he said. "Who knows what misfortune would befall you? No, *Señora*, you cannot go."

"I must go. I must know if the rumors are true or false. And no one will go for me."

"You have me."

"You? But you're—"

31

"Lame? I know I am lame," said Francisco. "I am only half a man. I find it difficult to walk or ride. Nevertheless, I will go and find word of *Don* Stanford. And when I do, I will return to Tumbalá immediately."

For six anxious days and nights Elodia waited for word from Francisco. When he failed to return on the seventh day, Elodia once again made preparations to leave Tumbalá for the day's journey to Ocosingo in search of her husband.

The morning dawned with characteristic heavy fog and drizzle, but by mid-morning a gentle wind began to break up the clouds that shrouded the mountain town. In a large white cloth Elodia wrapped two dozen tortillas, several hard-boiled eggs, a wedge of cheese, and some *pozole*—corn gruel. These she packed into her saddlebags, along with an extra change of clothes. After saddling her tan-colored riding mule, she led it onto the narrow street in front of her mother's house.

Too full of stress to weep, her mother implored the saints to guard and protect Elodia on her journey. Elodia kissed her mother's forehead, gave her a final hug, and placed her foot into the stirrup. As she was about to swing into the saddle, she heard the sound of barking dogs. She turned and gasped in disbelief. Like an apparition from a world beyond, Stanford strode out of the mist and down the cobblestone street into Elodia's outstretched arms.

In her excitement and joy, Elodia wanted to know the answers to a dozen questions. "What happened to Francisco? How did you get away from the soldiers? Were you hurt? Are you hungry? What's going to happen now?"

"My dear Lolita," chuckled Stanford. "I'll answer your

32

questions all in good time. First we must make plans to leave Tumbalá immediately. We can't even stay over-night at the *Alianza*. We must leave everything just as it is."

"Everything?"

"Everything. We'll take only what we can carry in our hands."

"Where are we going?" asked Elodia.

"New York!" he answered.

Stanford and Elodia's flight from the Chiapas high-lands took them four days of hard riding and river travel in a dugout canoe before they reached the port of Vera Cruz. On the way, Elodia learned that Stanford had been kept under house arrest in Ocosingo, confined to a small plaza where a half dozen soldiers guarded him.

Stanford apologized for not having sent word to her via Francisco. "I needed him," he explained.

"Needed him?"

"Yes, you know the custom in these small towns. With no relatives to help me, I needed him to buy food and bring it to me."

As Stanford explained the details surrounding his re-lease, it was difficult for Elodia to fully understand how the American consul in Mexico City could free her hus-band from a small village in the heart of Chiapas. But details weren't important to her. "All that matters is that we are together and we are going to the United States."

Stanford smiled and reassured his young wife that she was correct—everything was going to be all right. He didn't tell her why he believed the soldiers had released him without protest. He was sure they were planning to ambush him on the trail. Warned by a friend of this

33

strong possibility, Stanford did not follow the usual trail out of Tumbalá.

In spite of the threat, the difficult journey to Vera Cruz was without incident. There was, however, a moment at the dock in Vera Cruz when Elodia didn't know if she would ever walk up the gangplank of the ship that would take them to New York.

"Wait here on the dock with our bags," said Stanford. "I have a short errand in town. I'll be back within the hour. Then we'll go through customs and be on our way."

Elodia knew that the center of Vera Cruz was only a few blocks from the docks, and she welcomed a moment to catch her breath and observe all that was happening around her. Intrigued by the smells of salt water and creosoted pilings, and by the dock workers loading and unloading the ships, Elodia failed to notice a knot of soldiers who pointed after her husband and then to her.

"Hey *gringa!*" yelled a soldier as he gave her a sharp jab with the butt of his rifle.

For Elodia the next several minutes were tense and long as she was subject to their humiliating comments. With determination honed from years of hard mountain living, Elodia suppressed the tears that wanted to spill out and lowered her eyes from their greedy stares.

"Oh, come on, let's leave this country cousin to her *gringo* lover," interrupted one of the soldiers.

Laughing and making crude jokes among themselves, the soldiers sauntered off the dock and into the streets of Vera Cruz.

True to his word, Stanford returned within the hour. Surprised and confused when Elodia flung herself against his thick chest, Stanford asked what had happened while he had been gone.

"Nothing happened," said Elodia. She knew that if she told the truth, Stanford would become angry and go after the soldiers. All she wanted now was to get aboard ship and leave Mexico. "I'm just so happy you're back safely and we're truly going to New York."

Elodia's concept of New York had been formed by Stanford's description and by a dream she once had of the famous city. In her dream, Elodia had seen a city with tall buildings and hordes of people, but with an entrance so small it required her to become a dove in order to get in. In 1914, when she actually saw the New York skyline for the first time, she felt she was coming home.

For five happy, prosperous years, New York City was indeed home for the Morisons. Stanford's coffee import business did well, and Elodia was content. In fact, she would have been content to remain there for the rest of her life. But Stanford was not.

By 1918, the Mexican Revolution was beginning to acquire a purpose, and there was a measure of peace throughout the land. All this made Stanford restless to return to the land he could not get out of his blood.

Over Elodia's gentle protests, the Morisons returned to Mexico and the *Alianza* in 1920. Their house, as they had expected, had been ransacked. The coffee trees had been slashed, and the workers had fled. But with his customary determination and optimism, Stanford once again set out to establish himself in Mexico, and part of that establishment was to be his own progeny.

In 1921, Elodia bore a son they named Stannie. Two years later they had their first daughter—an energetic girl they named Mary. Six more children in almost as many years filled the Morison home: Rebecca, who also died at age three of pneumonia; Lolita, pretty but slightly retarded; Margarita, who for many years was frail and sickly; a second son, David, frail like his sister Margarita; Carmen and Blanca, adopted at age three.

"To a father waxing old, nothing is dearer than a daughter," wrote Euripides. From the beginning it was clear that Stanford and Mary had a special bond of love. Mary possessed a dash of impetuousness and lively energetic buoyancy. As a young teen-ager, with her long dark brown braids and soft brown eyes, Mary was irresistibly winsome to her father and to all who met her.

In her pre- and early teen years Stanford, along with his son Stannie, delighted in coming each morning to Mary's bedroom to awaken her. Then he would prepare a hearty breakfast of soft-boiled eggs and oatmeal. Mary loved her father, but not his American breakfast. As soon as Stanford left for the coffee processing building a short distance from the main house, Mary enjoyed a proper Mexican breakfast—tortillas, refried beans, black coffee, and sweet rolls.

Stanford loved to tell his friends about his football exploits, and since Mary had never seen this strange American game she never quite understood what her father was talking about. Her interests were different. She had a passion for parties, dances, and fiestas that brought its own kind of happiness into the Morison home, cushioning the hard reality of Stanford's cash flow problem. Through a series of bad debts, land redistribution, his own aging, and his persistent propensity to trust everyone (even employees who had their hands in the till), Stanford lost the *Esperanza* and the *Agua Azul* coffee ranches.

Elodia had known what it was to have little and to have much, and now, in 1940, she had little more than if she hadn't married Stanford. To keep the *Alianza* afloat, she and all able-bodied family members had to work. Mary sewed, scrubbed, ironed, and cooked the hand-ground corn for tortillas three times each day. If given permission, she went to parties in Yajalón and Tumbalá.

These parties were not just routine weekend parties. Elodia saw to it that her daughter attended only proper social functions of the community. In an unpretentious way, Elodia made Mary aware that she was different from the girls who hung out at dance halls. Her father was a respected gentleman, and she was his daughter. This meant Mary was to be properly chaperoned; she must also leave a party at a respectable hour; and under no circumstances was she to drink wine or any intoxicating drink.

Companionship was a much-needed element in the Morison household in 1940. Mary was almost seventeen, emerging into womanhood. And while she and Stannie had a deep affection for one another, there was a deep inner cry for fulfillment in Mary's life. The limits of her world were narrow. She had received some schooling in Tuxtla, and there had been tutors. But the tutors usually left after a few months due to her and Stannie's mischievous antics.

While Mary was an electric sparkler—a brisk, alive, determined young woman—she was also a deeply private person without friends or peers with whom she could fully identify. The girls at the parties were polite—too polite. Most kept Mary at a distance. After all, she was not quite like the rest of them. Her father was an American.

And for reasons unexplained, Mary could not identify with their all-consuming passion for fancy clothes, gossip, and the constant search for handsome men to marry. Marriage was the very last thing Mary wanted.

In a word, Mary was desperately lonely. At one point she felt so frustrated that she considered suicide the only way out. And when she learned Stannie was going north to join the U.S. Army, her private world took on an even greater despair.

Then, when everything seemed darkest for Mary, Stanford received a letter from a young man he had met and enjoyed on his visits to Yajalón. Charles William (Bill) Bentley, an American from Kansas, was studying the language of the Tzeltal Indians, a neighboring tribe to the Chol Indians who worked Stanford's coffee ranch. Bill, a square-jawed, handsome, outgoing young man had, like Stanford, studied pre-med. And like Stanford, he had come to Mexico to build.

But Bill had come to build a kingdom, not an empire. He explained that this kingdom would not be built with brick and mortar; it would be a spiritual kingdom brought into being by responsive faith in Jesus Christ.

"I admire your enthusiasm," Stanford said to Bill. "I was full of such energy when I was your age. But the Tzeltals are no ordinary people. They are proud, independent, and deeply suspicious of outsiders. They have a reputation for fighting and killing without provocation and, like the Chol people who live in this area, they have their own religion. I don't see how you are going to make Christians out of them."

"I don't intend to make them Christians," Bill assured him. "That's God's job. My job is to be His instrument and to obey Him. I believe God called me here to Mexico to learn the Tzeltal language and to translate the New Testament for the Tzeltal people."

Stanford could only smile and try his best to understand Bill's motives for giving his life to such a noble, but futile enterprise.

Stanford tried to explain to Elodia Bill's reasons for living in Mexico, but it just didn't make sense to her. They didn't really care, though. It was just pleasant to have Bill around when he came for a visit. There was a feeling of comfort and warmth in his voice and in his conversation.

When Bill spoke with anyone, he gave himself to the conversation with enthusiasm and interest. He was also thoughtful and kind. Stanford deeply enjoyed Bill's active mind and welcomed his fresh insight and intellectual stimulus.

After two years of a growing friendship with the Morison family, Bill sent Stanford a letter asking if two young American women—Evelyn Woodward and Marianna Slocum—could live on the *Alianza*.

"They're with the Summer Institute of Linguistics, the same organization as Bill's," Stanford told Elodia, "and they want to study the Chol language."

"Two young American girls and they want to live here and study the Chol language?" asked Elodia. "And what will they do after they learn to speak Chol?"

"They have a desire like Bill's—to translate the Bible, or at least the New Testament—for the Chols."

"How strange," mused Elodia. "I can't understand a word from that Bible you bought me. How can these Chol people, who have no books and cannot read, understand the Bible?"

"We'll just have to wait and see," said Stanford. "In the meantime, I'll send my answer to Bill."

CHAPTER THREE

The Invitation

Had it been 1900 instead of 1940, Marianna Slocum and her girlfriend Evelyn Woodward would have been perfect typecasts for illustrator Charles Gibson's famous Gibson Girl. His concept of the typical society woman was an attractive, athletic, poised, and intelligent woman.

Named after her two grandmothers—Mary and Anna—Marianna, at twenty-two, was slim with soft black shoulder-length hair and an open, responsive personality. She had graduated from high school with honors in French, and from Wilson College in Chambersburg, Pennsylvania *cum laude* and with special honors in English, Greek, Latin, and Hebrew. Marianna's flirtation with languages was to grow into a lifelong passion. She would write one day, "To me there is nothing in all the world more beautiful than a perfect verb pattern."

Her father, S. E. Slocum, besides being a godly Presbyterian elder, was a brilliant engineer who would win distinction for his invention of a special screw design for the famous liberty ships of World War II. From this scholarly, no-nonsense father and her fun-loving, gracious mother, Marianna learned all the proper graces, manners, and poise befitting anyone who lived in a three-story Victorian house and "dressed" for dinner.

Physically, Marianna was considered by her parents to be delicate. Before her first birthday, and again at age five, she almost died from severe attacks of flu. At age eleven she barely escaped death from scarlet fever. Yet in spite of her parents' perception of her health, Marianna became as proficient on horseback as she was conjugating a French verb.

Evelyn, like Marianna, came from a fine Philadelphia home. Her father had been an engineer in Mexico, and her grandfather had been a beloved country physician. Evelyn was also a student at Wilson College, and she too loved languages. But although she liked horses, she enjoyed music more.

Both of these young women experienced two profound personal awakenings. For Evelyn, the first awakening occurred at age sixteen. Marianna's came during her freshman year in college. This awakening allowed them to see a reality beyond what they had experienced with their five senses. They began a new spiritual life of trustful faith in God and His Son Jesus Christ. They were challenged to pattern their thinking and their conduct after God's will as revealed in the Scriptures.

The second awakening grew out of the first. It was an

awareness and desire to tell others that love, grace, beauty, patience, and compassion were all evidences of the character of God found in Jesus Christ, His Son. They had a zeal to serve God with the talents He had given them. From out of this new love relationship with God, they wanted to bring about a responsive faith and spiritual healing in people's lives, especially those who had never heard that God in love had come to humanity in the form of a baby.

After reading a small magazine called *The Wycliffe Chronicle* (then the official organ of the fledgling Wycliffe Bible Translators) that advertised special courses in linguistics for young people interested in translating the Bible for ethnic minorities, Marianna knew the pattern of her life was set. Now all that faced her, or so she thought, was to convince her father that this special "knowing" was from God.

"You want to go where and do what for the summer?" asked Mr. Slocum.

"To Sulphur Springs, Arkansas," answered Marianna. "I'm interested in a course of linguistic studies being offered by an organization called the Summer Institute of Linguistics. It's at Sulphur Springs, and it's called Camp Wycliffe. The teachers all work in Mexico with tribal peoples and come to the States during the summer to teach linguistics. I understand the facilities at the school are somewhat primitive—rather like camping."

"And what do you propose to do after your three months of linguistic studies at this Camp Wycliffe?"

"I believe the Lord would have me join this organization to do Bible translation work in Mexico."

"You mean you are willing to turn your back on a

brilliant academic future to work among a primitive group of people in the jungles of Mexico?"

"Yes," said Marianna simply. "I am."

"But that's absurd! You're not strong enough. Think of your health. How do you expect to survive in such primitive conditions? Besides, what do we know about this Summer Institute of Linguistics?"

"Well, it was started by William Cameron Townsend, and it currently has thirty members.* You know Professor Strevig from Wilson, and you know what a godly person she is."

"Yes, indeed I do," said Mr. Slocum.

"She first suggested the Summer Institute to me. She's also a personal friend of L. L. Legters, the cofounder of the Summer Institute."

"And this other gentleman—Mr. Townsend—where has he already translated the Bible for tribal people?"

"Guatemala. He and his wife worked as missionaries there for ten years."

"Well, my dear Marianna, I believe it most courageous of you to want to affiliate yourself with this group of people, who are no doubt very dedicated. But to go to a foreign country just on faith, without financial support or backing of a proper board of directors or sponsorship of a large church, seems to me to be most insecure, and if I may say so, a suicidal venture. But I know if you feel God directing, you must go."

During the summer of 1940, President Franklin Delano Roosevelt was assuring the American public, "Our boys are not going to be sent into any foreign wars." Marianna, attending the Summer Institute of Linguistics at Sulphur Springs, was sending home her own

*See page 155.

soothing messages of assurance. To ease her parents' apprehensions about her future, Marianna wrote glowing reports about the tribal people to whom she felt God leading her.

Curiously, Marianna's letters also included the oft-repeated name of one Bill Bentley.

Dearest Folks:

My dear friend Evy (Evelyn Woodward) I told you about in my last letter (she's also a graduate from Wilson but a couple of years ahead of me) and I feel the Lord directing us to work together with a Mayan tribe in the state of Chiapas. They're called the Chols. Chiapas, by the way, is a southern state in Mexico and adjoins Guatemala.

One of the young linguists I've met here at Camp Wycliffe is Bill Bentley, a very outgoing and beautifully dedicated fellow. He has worked for two years among the Tzeltal people. They are an adjoining tribe to the Chols.

From Bill I learned the Chols live in a very lovely and healthful part of the state—about 2,000 to 4,000 feet. There are also many coffee ranches in the region run by Germans and Americans. It's on one of these ranches owned by an American—a Yale graduate—that Bill thinks Evelyn and I will be able to stay. Bill says there is a large number of Chol speakers right on the ranch.

While Mrs. Slocum exclaimed over Marianna's positive and enthusiastic letters, Mr. Slocum dug out a map of Mexico and examined the state of Chiapas. "Marianna failed to mention that two-thirds of the state is unexplored territory!" he exclaimed.

"That doesn't matter," said Mrs. Slocum. "Listen to

what else your daughter has written. It looks like she'll be well looked after by this young Bill Bentley!"

> Bill is a grand fellow. He reminds me of brother Walter in his looks and personality. He has promised to go with us all the way to our destination and get us settled.
>
> I am enclosing Bill's comments on the tribes that are available for us to work in, advantages of each tribe, etc. Let me know your comments. But be assured that we are not going into this work blindly. We have prayed a great deal about this and are using sanctified common sense. Of all the tribes we have looked into, the Chols look the best to us, and besides, we feel the Lord's leading and direction more to this tribe than to any other.

And so it was settled. Marianna and Evelyn each had ninety dollars (one month's support) and a one-way train ticket to the wilds of Mexico. (Marianna's ninety dollars was a gift from her brother.)

Mr. Slocum had unabashedly overprotected Marianna as she grew up. After all, he reasoned, she had begun life with extreme fragility, and it was his responsibility to protect her. Therefore, when he understood that his supposedly frail daughter possessed an iron will and meant to go directly to Mexico after Camp Wycliffe, he responded characteristically. He and his wife drove from Philadelphia to Sulphur Springs for one last attempt to comprehend this madness that captivated his refined and delicate daughter.

Of that trip Mr. Slocum later wrote in his journal:

> It was a long four-day drive to Sulphur Springs, made longer because we both felt we were losing our daughter

forever. When we finally arrived at this Camp Wycliffe, I must confess I was not prepared for what I found. The facilities were primitive in the extreme!

But when Mrs. Slocum and I met Cameron Townsend and saw and felt the enthusiasm of these young pioneers, we began to change our minds toward this group. In fact, after observing the godly dedication of these young people, we were so inspired it revolutionized our thinking. All at once the physical hardships seemed trivial.

However, when we saw the old truck the Summer Institute had hired to carry the young people and their luggage to Mexico, we decided to drive Marianna, Evelyn, and another girl to Mexico City. We would have been happy to have driven them all the way to Chiapas, but there were no roads. They had to rely on the train for their transport.

In the true tradition of one from the old school, Mr. Slocum carefully guarded his deep, innermost feelings from public view. However, a single sentence from his journal eloquently and poignantly revealed the depth of his concern for his beloved daughter. "When at last we reached Mexico City," he wrote, "we were compelled to part with her who had been the object of our loving care since infancy." From that moment until his death, it was said of Mr. Slocum that he never drank a glass of water but that he prayed for Marianna.

In every way it was the most courteous of letters, quite within the normal experience of the etiquette that Marianna and Evelyn were accustomed to. It was addressed to Bill Bentley.

47

NEVER TOUCH A TIGER

Tumbalá, Chiapas, Mexico
La Alianza, Sept. 4, 1940

Dear Mr. Bentley:

Your letter of August 20th reached me yesterday afternoon. Mrs. Morison and I are delighted to hear that the two young ladies you mentioned are coming down here with you.

My judgment about the matter, since you are good enough to ask for it, is that as soon as convenient after reaching Yajalón, you bring them to the *Alianza* to visit for as long as you and they wish. This is a much better place to learn the Chol language and also it will be a great pleasure to us to have all three of you with us, and especially to Mary I am sure.

Please let us know by telephone from Yajalón a few days ahead of when you all can come here, telling us how many *cargadores* (mules and drivers to carry supplies and baggage) you need and we will try to send them as promptly as possible.

With best regards.

Yours sincerely,
(Signed) Stanford N. Morison

Marianna and Evelyn, of course, had no idea what lay ahead of them. They knew only that God seemed to be leading them and adding a new and exciting dimension to their lives, and that this was yet another example of His unique provision for their needs. Yet they felt they should consider other alternatives before accepting Mr. Morison's gracious invitation. It wasn't that the young women were ungrateful; it was just that so much was happening around them that it was difficult to make a choice. One of their first exciting experiences was the train trip to Tuxtla.

The trip was actually in three stages. The first began on a night train in Mexico City. It took them to Vera Cruz, a distance of less than two hundred miles, but the trip lasted eighteen hours! It was eighteen hours of sitting and trying to sleep on hard, second-class lacquered slatted bench seats; eighteen hours of stops and starts, of jerks and jolts; eighteen hours of sharing the coach with crying babies and passengers who packed their chickens under the lacquered seats. It was also eighteen hours of hot dusty air mixed with grimy soot from the engine blowing in from open windows. Yet after this part of their journey, Marianna, Evelyn, and Bill were less than halfway to their destination.

After staying overnight in the tropical port city of Vera Cruz (in a third-class hotel), the little party started the second phase of their journey. Their destination was Tuxtla, at the end of the railroad line and less than two hundred miles away. Had there been roads, a bus could have made it in six to eight hours. But it took them two nights and a day.

And when they reached Tuxtla, there was still a grueling overland horseback ride to Las Casas in the mountains, plus another long hard ride to Yajalón, and a further five- to six-hour ride to the *Alianza*. The trip from Tuxtla to the *Alianza* could take as long as six to seven days.

Yet with all her journeying, Marianna wrote that she had fallen in love with Mexico, particularly the subtropics. And as Mr. and Mrs. Slocum read Marianna's long and exhaustive letter, they realized that Mexico was not the only thing their daughter had fallen in love with.

NEVER TOUCH A TIGER

Dearest Folks:

As you know, we arrived here on October 12—Mexico's Day of the Indian. This is a special day set apart to celebrate Indian heritage. Seems rather prophetic that we two greenhorns who want to work among the Indian tribes should have arrived on this important day.

I got my week's mail—four grand letters from you—handed up to me on muleback last Friday morning as we were about to leave on our all-day trip to Tumbalá. So I rode off into the mountains, in full tropical sunlight, reading how it has snowed at home and about that write-up in the Philadelphia paper. I was especially interested in the headline, "Philadelphia Girls Brave Bugs and Beans"!

I'm certainly thankful for the true testimony it bears for the Lord Jesus. And it's not far from wrong on such minor points as bugs (200 or so bites per person at first, but they're not bothering us at all now) and beans (much as I like black Mexican beans, they don't like me).

We can't help but laugh at the hardships people consider us to be undergoing. They forget the Lord's grace is abundantly sufficient for everything we are experiencing. Furthermore, we honestly count it all joy to have been chosen by the Lord to come here. And I can never thank the Lord enough for a dearly loved mother and dad who also love Him, and who want His saving grace to be known by others.

Well, Evy and I are about ready to be classed as old residents now after two weeks in this town. We're mighty proud to be inhabitants of the state of Chiapas. I don't believe there could be any lovelier scenery in the world than our Chiapas mountains. There is nothing more picturesque than the trails leading off through groves of bananas, and sugar cane patches that lead to the thatched huts of the Indians. The climate is ideal—clear, warm sunlight and blue skies filled with white clouds almost every day, and since this is their rainy season, brief rains wash the countryside every afternoon.

We are comfortable here in our spacious rooms with the clean brick floors, whitewashed walls, and beam ceilings. There is a profusion of lovely flowers blooming in the courtyard and, beyond a large cement floor where they spread coffee beans to dry in the sun, there is a rushing river.

Evy and I are using Bill's one-burner stove to make our breakfast of hot milk with cinnamon, sugar rolls, and fruit. Our pressure cooker is a true Godsend and fun to use. We use it to cook lunch at *Doña* Molly Rasmussen's—a Norwegian widow with two sons in the States and two young daughters here. She has lived in Mexico for twenty-six years, speaks English, and is a big help to us. We have supper in our rooms—usually fruit and sweet bread.

We have begun studying the Chol language with a real smart Chol woman—María, about thirty-five, who speaks Spanish as well as Chol. We love her and love to work on the language. We can only study an hour a day because María works for one of the believers who has loaned her to us free of charge for this time. It's quite a feat to be studying two languages at once, but Christ is our wisdom. Pray that we may soon learn both of them well, to His glory.

Our first week here in Yajalón, *Doña* Emilia Setzer, the German lady at whose coffee ranch Bill has been living for the past two years, sent Bill down with mules to take us up there. We had a grand two-hour ride up the mountain to her *finca* (coffee ranch). The ranch, set against the mountains, is perfectly lovely and looks like a Swiss chalet—the kind you see in movies. We stayed overnight. *Doña* Emilia gave us Bill's lovely attic room.

We fully enjoyed the marvelous German food—five

meals a day! Coffee, bread, jam, and cakes as soon as you get up. Breakfast is at nine with meat, eggs, cereal, coffee, etc. Dinner is at two, all courses. At 4:30 we have coffee and cake etc., and supper is at 7:00.

Doña Emilia herself is quite a character. She was born in Russia, traveled all over Europe, hid a fugitive soldier in her closet in Italy, has been governess to Vanderbilts, Morgans, and the Four Hundred of New York society, has a rascally husband who can't (she hopes) get out of Germany, and has a picture of Hitler dominating the dining room! She is unceasingly, boundlessly generous, and has a keen sense of humor. And such adventures she has had!

During a lull in one of the Indian uprisings here, she livened things up by having one of her Indian servants set a row of signal fires on the brow of the mountain overlooking the town of Yajalón. The inhabitants expected the Indians to descend upon them from the mountains and, extremely frightened, set to work blockading the streets.

And then on Friday we departed again—this time for an all-day ride to Tumbalá and to Mr. Morison's coffee ranch. He is a tall, elderly man, a "gentleman of the old school," a graduate of Exeter Academy and Yale, and a member of Walter Camp's invincible Yale football team of '91. He has lived here forty-six years running various coffee ranches and has been through Indian uprisings and the Revolution. Once he was forced to quarter 150 soldiers. He married a Mexican woman about twenty years younger than he.

He comes from a fine family in the Midwest and has a library of over 1,000 books, including the *Encyclopedia Britannica.* His uncle, Stanford Newell, was U.S. ambassador to Holland before the World War. We've eaten off monogrammed plates with which Queen Wilhelmina herself had been served!

From the large porch of the ranch house there is a wonderful view of the Chiapas mountains, the lowlands of the state of Tabasco, and with good eyesight and a telescope you can see the gulf.

Mr. Morison and his wife and children were very cordial to us, and after visiting the *Alianza,* we feel it's the Lord's leading for us to live there. There is a tiny house which the foreman used to live in down by the *beneficio* (coffee washing building). It's up on stilts, about as big as a minute, and has a tin roof. It's about a hundred yards from the ranch house and has a little stream running behind. There is a wonderful view, the climate is perfect (elevation 4,000 feet), Indian houses are within walking distance, as is the town of Tumbalá where there is already a small congregation of Chol Christians who hold services in pure Chol. They're also waiting for God's Word in their own language.

Mr. Morison has a dictionary of over 1,000 Chol words. Since he has Indians working in his fields, he has learned to speak Chol, as does most of his family.

We are looking to the Lord to supply us with a native Chol speaker who will teach us the language. We plan to move up to the *Alianza* next weekend. When we get there, we'll have a room at the ranch house at first, and take our meals with the Morisons until we get settled in our own place.

Bill will only be about a three- or four-hour walk from us. I can't tell you how perfectly wonderful he has been through all these days and all the miles we have traveled. The love of Christ is continually manifested in him. He is always thinking of others. There is an old woman in Tuxtla who is almost blind and he bought her a self-threading needle. He brought back some tea for *Doña* Rasmussen as it's expensive and hard to get here in Mexico.

Whenever we go on a trip by mule, Bill never rides. He always walks the trails on foot, taking care of us and the mules, speaking Spanish for us, making all the arrangements, always being sweet and thoughtful. Evy wonders how he can possibly keep walking after thirteen hours on the muddy, slippery trail, but he does. Did I tell you he has a beautiful singing voice and a beautiful, winsome smile? Everyone likes Bill. They say he will do anything for anyone.

In closing let me tell what it was like when we arrived at the *Alianza*. It was Friday night about 6:30. We traveled the last few leagues with our ponchos on as there was a torrential downpour. But even though it was wet and cold we enjoyed the gorgeous vegetation of feathery tree ferns.

The young Morison daughter, Mary, and her brother Stannie rode out to meet us on the trail. There was a grand turkey dinner waiting for us and Mr. Morison regaled us with his adventures here in Mexico and on the Yale football team.

I want to let you know that the Lord wonderfully supplies me with strength for these trips (2 Corinthians 12:9,10). Part of the promise of these verses is that "when I am weak, then I am strong. The less I have the more I depend on Him."

Well, I have covered about everything. Send my mail now to Tumbalá. Keep well, and dearest love to you all. Pray for the Morison children, especially Mary. She is the only one who doesn't seem to be interested in coming to a Sunday school class that Evy and I want to start.

You are in my prayers and in my heart always.

Toots.

CHAPTER FOUR

A Bold New World

"Why so sad?" said Stannie, pinching Mary's dimpled cheek. "Today's your birthday! You're seventeen—time to find yourself a husband."

"Stop teasing me," said Mary, brushing his hand aside. "I'm not the least interested in getting married— now or maybe ever! All the girls I know who got married at fourteen or fifteen are just slaves for their husbands—and that's not for me!"

"Your temper is showing," said Stannie with a broad, impish smile. "If you don't want to get married, what do you want to do?"

"I don't know," said Mary. "I'm so confused. You're leaving soon to join the American army and when you go, there will be no one to talk to or have fun with. I know Father loves me, but he says there's no money to send me to school. And Mother has been sick and there's always too much work for her to do."

"Mother's not the only one who works hard. From sunup to sunset all I ever see my little sister do is work—and such a fast worker, too!"

"Now you're teasing me again," said Mary, with a quiet smile.

"Hey, what about Marianna and Evelyn? Why don't you talk to them about how you feel?"

"I notice *you* like to talk to Evelyn."

"It's because she can speak Spanish and has some interesting things to say about God."

"I think she talks too much about God," said Mary. "She hasn't stopped talking about God and Jesus since she arrived! I like them, and Mother says our house has been happier since they came, but I think both of them are too fanatical about their religion. Remember when they first came, how they asked us to come and sing songs and hear a story from the Bible every afternoon?"

"Margarita and the rest seem to enjoy it . . ."

"Well not me. I refused to go to their little meeting, and I also refused a Bible they wanted me to have."

"Why didn't you take it? You don't have to accept their religion."

To Marianna and Evelyn, Mary appeared self-assured and confident. Yet down deep, Mary felt an overwhelming sense of inner loneliness and social isolation. Furthermore, her seventeenth birthday, instead of being a day of celebration, emphasized the growing realization that her life held no meaning. Without the possibility of further schooling, she felt stuck on the margins of life, alienated from her peers and even from her own culture.

When she tried to explain all this to Marianna and

Evelyn over breakfast one morning, she suddenly broke into tears. But then, just as suddenly, Mary clasped her hand over her mouth and ran from their presence.

Later, in the privacy of their tin-roofed house, Marianna and Evelyn discussed Mary's behavior.

"You know," said Marianna, "Bill told me he felt a strange burden for Mary. One of the reasons he was anxious for us to come to the *Alianza* was for Mary's sake. He felt we could have a positive ministry in her life."

"And all the time I thought it was so Bill could be close to you," teased Evelyn.

"What do you mean?" said Marianna with fake indignation. "Bill hasn't said a thing to me. I don't know if he even thinks of me romantically. I'm probably like a sister to him."

"He doesn't have to say a word to you," said Evelyn knowingly. "I can tell he likes you, and deep down so can you. Anyway, I agree with Bill. We should try to encourage Mary all we can, especially to help her see how much she is loved by us—and by God."

On the first night of their arrival at the *Alianza*, Marianna and Evelyn had slipped to their knees in prayer. "Lord," they had prayed, "You haven't brought us four thousand miles for nothing. We pray for the salvation of every member of this family."

Implicit in this prayer was their desire for each one to understand that all of God's character and nature were revealed in Jesus Christ and that they could begin to enjoy true peace and fellowship with God through a decisive change of will. In a word, Marianna and Evelyn were praying for the Morison family to be converted to a life of trustful faith in Jesus Christ that would enable them to model their thinking and conduct after Him.

Yet Mary, her loneliness notwithstanding, stoutly refused to listen to the gospel story or to confess to God her desperate need for wholeness, meaning, and reality.

As the weeks passed, Marianna and Evelyn gave themselves diligently to language study. They made friends among the Chols and grew increasingly fond of the Morison family. Marianna waited anxiously and expectantly for Bill's fortnightly visits.

Stanford enjoyed a rekindling of his old school chivalry. Graciously he saw to Marianna's and Evelyn's physical needs by providing mules and guides whenever they visited surrounding Chol villages.

Elodia marveled at their charm and how warm and good she felt inside whenever she was around them. But she also marveled at their naiveté.

On one occasion, after Marianna and Evelyn had unsuccessfully treated a Chol woman who had complained of stomach pains, they brought her to Elodia.

"This woman has complained for two days about pains in her stomach," said Marianna.

"Yes," added Evelyn, "and we've given her worm medicine and some other things, and still she doesn't seem to be any better."

After scarcely looking at the Chol woman, Elodia merrily announced her prognosis. "Of course this woman is having stomach pains. She's going to have a baby!"

Elodia was not the only person who realized that Marianna and Evelyn were innocents abroad. Cameron Townsend (Uncle Cam) rode into the *Alianza* one January afternoon during a thunderous rainstorm. Uncle Cam's purpose in visiting Marianna and Evelyn was to help the young translators with their linguistic field work and to encourage them and assure them that they were not forgotten.

The visit was short—just a couple of days to meet the Morisons and to better acquaint himself with the Chol and Tzeltal translation problems and opportunities. But this brief visit would trigger a most significant and far-reaching turn of events in the months and years to come.

On February 14, that special day when, according to English poet Geoffrey of Monmouth, "birds begin to pair off," Bill Bentley hiked over a thin, muddy mountain trail from Tzeltal country and settled once and for all Marianna's romantic anxieties.

Remarkably free from affectation, Bill and Marianna would have been content with a simple wedding ceremony in a humble church or chapel. But at the request of Marianna's parents that they not be denied the special joy of this splendid moment, Marianna and Bill decided to return to Philadelphia to be married.

The date was set for Saturday, August 27. Marianna, Bill, and Evelyn would leave Mexico in May and go to Sulphur Springs, where they would participate in the Summer Institute of Linguistics program. Then Marianna and Bill would go to her home to prepare for their wedding.

But several weeks before Marianna and Evelyn were to leave the *Alianza*, a letter from Uncle Cam threw their neat plans into disarray.

"Listen to this," said Marianna. "Uncle Cam suggests we take Mary back with us to the States."

"Whatever for?" asked Evelyn.

"So she can go to school and get an education."

"But who will pay for this? I can't on the thirty dollars

a month I get for support. And I don't think the Morisons have money. Stannie told me he thinks his father might even lose the *Alianza*."

"That's not all," said Marianna. "Uncle Cam suggests further that since I'm going to be married and you will need a new partner, perhaps Mary would be great for you."

"That's absurd!" sputtered Evelyn. "Mary hasn't shown the slightest interest in spiritual things. If anything, she's quite disinterested in everything I've tried to tell her about the Lord."

"I agree," said Marianna. "We'll just drop the subject. Perhaps he'll forget about it."

In the world of men, there are those who through the force of their dreams and ideas become larger than themselves. Cameron Townsend was not only larger than himself; in remarkable ways he was larger than the two worldwide organizations he founded—the Summer Institute of Linguistics and Wycliffe Bible Translators.

Marianna and Evelyn began to perceive this great strength when they received a second letter just six days before they were to leave the *Alianza*. In his customary fashion of never giving a direct order to a subordinate, Uncle Cam wondered if the young women had prayed about taking Mary with them to the States. If they hadn't, he kindly suggested they ask the Lord for clear direction.

"You know," said Evelyn, "we really haven't asked the Lord about taking Mary. I know having her along will be a little awkward and we'll have to pool our pennies, but what do you think?"

Marianna agreed. "Uncle Cam is our director and if, after just meeting Mary once, he feels this strongly that she should get an education, the least we can do is pray about it."

And so they did. The following morning both women awoke, and for a few moments they looked at each other in knowing silence. "Of course," said Marianna at last. "I know it's right to take Mary to the States."

"That's exactly the way I feel, too," Evelyn excitedly agreed. "I don't know how or why, but I just feel the Lord impressing upon me that it's His will for Mary to come with us."

"Now all that remains," Marianna mused, "is for us to get the Morisons' permission, persuade Mary to leave home—"

"—Choose a school, and find the money for room, board, tuition, and clothes," finished Evelyn.

"But isn't this what faith is all about?" asked Marianna. "I have no idea where the money will come from, but I know it's right to take Mary to get an education.

Marianna and Evelyn had seen jubilant young people before. On occasion, they had even been jubilant young people! But never had they seen anyone explode into wilder enthusiasm than Mary did when they asked if she would like to go with them to the States.

"Oh, Mother! Mother!" cried Mary. "The girls—they want to take me to the United States and put me through school."

"Really? Is this really true? Did they say this?" asked Elodia, wiping her hands on her white apron. "You know we don't have any finances—none at all."

"Marianna and Evelyn said we didn't have to worry about money. They would pay for my schooling."

"Is this really true? Are you sure this is what they said? You know they don't speak Spanish too well."

"Yes, yes, it's true! I understood them clearly," said Mary with tears in her eyes.

"Oh, my Mary, my Mary." Elodia fell weeping into Mary's arms.

"The girls leave here in five days. Will I be able to go with them?" asked Mary.

"Of course you will go with them," said Elodia. "Your father is in Yajalón until tomorrow and it's a good thing he is. He's so proud and probably won't want you to go. But I'll speak to him. This is an opportunity you must take."

"But what about their religion?" asked Mary.

"Listen to me," said Elodia. "When Marianna and Evelyn first came to live here they told me I should accept Jesus Christ into my life. But I thought if your father's religion is good enough for him, it's good enough for me. I don't know what they have, but somehow what they believe makes them different from any religious person I have ever met. These young women brought a new hope and purity to this house. I enjoy being around them.

"And have you looked at Bill? Your father said in all his life he's never seen a man treat a woman as kindly and purely as Bill treats Marianna. I've seen this, too. If ever I saw a walking saint it's Bill Bentley. I think even his thoughts are pure.

"Mary, whatever it is they have, it won't hurt you to be around them. Besides, there is another reason I am happy for you to go."

"What is that?" asked Mary.

"It's the *Alianza*," said Elodia. "We are going to lose the ranch."

Two days later, Stanford asked Marianna and Evelyn

to come in for afternoon tea. Casually he chatted about his trip to Yajalón, lamenting that he did not have the money to buy a pool table he fancied there. Then, sitting upright in his overstuffed chair, he said, "My wife tells me you would like to take Mary away to the States for schooling."

"Yes," they said, "and we would like your permission."

"You understand I wouldn't be able to give anything toward it financially?"

"We understand," said Marianna. "All we want is your permission."

There was a wistful look on his face. He sniffed as he brushed his nose with the knuckle of his index finger and said simply, "She may go."

Marianna had told Evelyn not to worry about finances—God would provide. He did, but not the way Marianna had envisioned. When the two women and Bill pooled their money and divided it four ways, they had only enough for train fare from Tuxtla to Mexico City. Once there, they would need additional funds to take them on to Sulphur Springs.

"It's obvious we can't fly out of Yajalón," said Bill. "This means we'll have to go overland to Las Casas. It should only take three days."

Bill was right. It was only a three-day trip, but what a trip! On horses and mules provided by Mr. Morison, the little band that now included Bill's friend from Yucatán, Brainard Legters,* set out for the town of Las Casas in a tropical rainstorm. Hour after hour, with rain splattering into their eyes and down their necks, they moved up one mountainside and down the next, often covering

---

*Son of L. L. Legters, co-founder (with Cameron Townsend) of Wycliffe Bible Translators.

only a mile or two an hour on the narrow switchback trails. About that never-to-be-forgotten experience Evelyn wrote:

The dry season ended abruptly at noon the day we left. Marianna and I had coats, as did Mary and Brainard, but Bill didn't and was quickly drenched to the skin.

I don't know how many miles we traveled that first day. The country is terribly rugged and the trails are like corkscrews. You can walk a mile and be only three blocks from where you started.

At two in the afternoon we arrived in the small village of Chilón. Only a few families live there in small stick huts. It was obvious there was no place for us to stay. Finally Bill talked to a family and they graciously vacated their room where we girls could have some privacy.

The room was small, barely big enough to accommodate a narrow single bed (no mattress, just wooden) and a small child's bed, also without a mattress. Marianna quickly crawled up on the child's bed, and Mary and I slept full length on the narrow single bed.

Bill didn't have a change of clothes, so Brainard lent him his pajamas while Bill's clothes dried over a smoky open fire.

The next day I was saddlesore and stiff, and not the least happy with the thought of two more days of trail travel. Mary, on the other hand, was as happy and limber as if she were going to a party.

Just about dusk on the second day, after traveling since dawn, we reached a town that had a terrible reputation for drunkenness and killing. Since we knew many of the men in the village would kill for just a few pesos, we decided to press on as far as we could go. Just when it became too dark to go any further, we came to a bluff and camped for the night.

We were cold and hungry and thirsty. There had been

no place along the way where we could get food. We had taken some tortillas along from the *Alianza* but these were now all gone. Somewhere along the way Marianna had picked up some eggs. Gallantly she made a little fire and tried to roast hers, but it exploded. I ate mine raw. That night we all slept on the trail in our sleeping bags to dream of warm beds, coffee filled with hot milk, black beans, and sizzling steaks. Fortunately, we didn't have to wait too long for our dreams to come true. The next afternoon we finally reached the high country and the town of Las Casas.

After the little group reached Tuxtla, things moved rapidly. Mary visited and said good-bye to an aunt. When the aunt asked why Mary was leaving Mexico, Mary said simply, "Mother always told us we should go to the United States if we had the opportunity. I'm so excited. Somehow I feel my life will never be the same again."

Mary had no idea how prophetic her words were. Almost overnight she entered a bold, new, exciting world, a world where every turn meant a new discovery. White tie-shoes replaced her sandles, and store-bought dresses replaced the ones Elodia had made from calico prints. Later, after reaching Arkansas, Mary found that Evelyn expected her to learn and speak English. As an added bonus, Evelyn would teach her how to type.

While Mary was in Mexico City, in preparation for the trip to SIL (Summer Institute of Linguistics) in Arkansas, she had yet another surprise.

"You know, Mary," said Evelyn, "most people your age have already had four years of high school. Since you've only had a sixth-grade education, you will have to be in class with children much younger than yourself.

"Marianna and I don't know how you feel about this,

but we thought for your first school year, to help you get adjusted and learn English better, you could attend a school in Albany, New York. We have friends at this school and they will love and help you all they can. But it's a Bible school. Would you be willing to go to this kind of school?"

"Oh, yes," said Mary with characteristic enthusiasm. "I'll be happy to go to this school."

And when Mary finally reached SIL in Sulphur Springs and began to make friends, she was to make the ultimate discovery. Of those first weeks at SIL, Evelyn recalls the following:

> Since Mary was going to go to a Bible school, we bought her a diglot New Testament (Spanish and English). When we explained she could follow along in Spanish when someone was reading in English and that it would help her learn English, she accepted it without protest.
>
> Marianna stayed at SIL until mid-July, then left with Bill to prepare for their wedding.
>
> Mary roomed with me but I encouraged her to become acquainted with as many people as she could. She became good friends with Lulu Reber and Georgina Hammond, missionaries from Colombia, who were fluent in Spanish and roomed next door. From the moment Mary realized Georgina and Lulu could speak Spanish, the three were inseparable.
>
> Mary possessed then, and does now, a special blend of liveliness and charm with just a dash of audaciousness that endears her to all who meet her. And on her first Sunday at SIL, someone, believing Mary to have a personal trust in Jesus Christ as her Savior, asked her to speak at a Spanish Sunday school. It was my first look into Mary's heart.

Speaking in Spanish with Georgina translating, Mary told how excited she was when her father told her about the two young American girls coming to live on their ranch. "I was overjoyed to have someone my own age to talk with, someone who understood what only girls understand," said Mary. "But I could not understand why they were coming."

Then Mary told us all about her grandfather who had died from drunkenness, about the pain her mother went through after the death of her father. She explained how she never felt fully accepted by the other Mexican girls because she was considered an outsider from the coffee plantation. And then she told how most of her peers had gotten married early and of the pressure for her to do the same. "But I wasn't going to become a slave to any man," she said.

Shortly after that Sunday I came into our room and found Mary reading her New Testament. "I like it here very much," she said. "I don't know when I have been happier. Everyone likes me; they seem to understand me and accept me."

"Of course we accept you," I said. "We all love you."

And then Mary said something that made me realize that a spiritual awakening was beginning in her young life. "I have never seen young men so kind and gentlemanly," said Mary. "I see something different in the lives of these men. Georgina and I have been talking and she has been explaining that God is a gentleman who respects my freedom and who won't force Himself into my life. I'm beginning to believe this."

Then, something occurred that had a profound effect on Mary and on all the staff and students at SIL, and for a great many people around the world.

It was Sunday morning, August 21, 1941. Uncle Cam received a phone call from Marianna's father. Mr.

Slocum said quietly, "I have the painful duty to inform you, sir, that during the early morning hours Bill Bentley succumbed to a heart attack. He is dead. Marianna is on the line and would like to speak with you."

CHAPTER FIVE

Turning Points

The wedding invitations had been sent out; Marianna's dress was receiving its final fitting; and the florist, violinist, minister, best man, and bridesmaids all had been selected. Some early wedding presents had come, and Mrs. Slocum had put them on display in the large Victorian drawing room.

The mood in the Slocum household was happy, relaxed, and peaceful. In fact, Marianna felt so relaxed and prepared that she took Bill, his best man, and a friend from Yucatán to see the big city of New York.

They returned in great spirits and filled with the kind of joy that happy, secure children display—spontaneous and innocent. There was an air of easy communication that each could feel and understand without having to speak. The thought of Bill and Marianna's wedding, exactly a week away, made the present time all the more pleasurable.

To top off a perfect day Bill, with his characteristic thoughtfulness, bought a carton of ice cream to share with Mr. and Mrs. Slocum. That was on Saturday night.

The next morning Bill did not appear for breakfast. "He's probably overtired from the trip to New York," said Mr. Slocum. "Let's not disturb him." But as it drew near the time to leave for church and Bill still hadn't made an appearance, Mr. Slocum walked up the winding staircase and called him.

There was no response.

With a gentle knock, Mr. Slocum opened the bedroom door and peeked inside. The shades were pulled down, but Mr. Slocum could see the outline of Bill's body under the bedclothes. "He's a hard fellow to wake," thought Mr. Slocum as he walked over to the bed. But looking closer, he knew why Bill hadn't responded to his call.

Stunned, all Mr. Slocum could say was, "He's gone." Within twenty minutes, two physicians arrived and explained to the shocked Slocum household that sometime during the early morning Bill had suffered a heart attack. After the doctors learned that Bill had spent the past three years in Chiapas, they concluded that his hikes over the rugged mountain trails had been too much for a heart left weak from childhood rheumatic fever.

With evident sincerity Marianna said, "The Lord hath given and the Lord hath taken away; blessed be the name of the Lord." And as she repeated these solemn words to reaffirm her faith and confidence in the Lord, Marianna reached a decision. "Dad," she said slowly, "please phone Uncle Cam."

"Uncle Cam, this is Marianna. My father has told you about Bill . . ."

"Yes, and I'm so very sorry."

"Uncle Cam, will you let me take Bill's place among the Tzeltals? I want to return to Mexico immediately and continue his work."

It was an impossible request, but it was equally impossible to refuse. Later, Uncle Cam tried to persuade Marianna to consider another assignment. "The Tzeltals are one of Mexico's most difficult and dangerous groups," he told her. But although she was fragile and soft-spoken, Marianna's intensity prevailed.

When Marianna said she wanted to return to Mexico immediately, she meant exactly that. Three days later, the minister who was to have married Bill and Marianna conducted Bill's funeral. For the minister and the many who attended, it was a never-to-be-forgotten spiritual experience.

Marianna's thoughts were veiled. Scarcely believing what was happening, she sat tearless beside Bill's casket, unconsciously twisting her wedding ring around and around on her finger (a ring she continued to wear for many years).

After the funeral, Marianna and her brother accompanied Bill's body on a train to Topeka, Kansas, his home town. There he was buried.

On Saturday, the day she was to have become Mrs. Bentley, Marianna was back at SIL in Sulphur Springs, Arkansas. She requested that she be allowed to spend the day alone in her room—with her Lord and her memories. It was there, for the first time, that the dam broke.

Then, for the second time in twelve months, Mr. Slocum drove Marianna back to Mexico City. Before she left Sulphur Springs, she spoke to Mary and encouraged her to make the most of her year in Bible school. Marianna knew Mary was fond of Bill, and she told her that one of the last conversations she had with Bill was about her.

"Bill was deeply fond of you and was burdened for you spiritually. Now Evelyn tells me you have indeed accepted Jesus Christ into your life."

Mary, with her limited understanding of what was taking place in her spiritual life, said that she had. Now she was praying for her family, especially Stannie.

"God is faithful and in his own time will answer your prayers," Marianna told her. "When I see your mother and father, I'll explain as best I can how you have entered into this new relationship with Jesus Christ."

In his journal Mr. Slocum wrote: "Her sister and I drove to Camp Wycliffe to pick Marianna up and then drove her to Mexico City. It was all we could do for her. And from there she went her lonely way back to the mountains of Chiapas."

But things were not as they appeared. True, Marianna was lonely and still bewildered over the unexpected turn of events, but she was not defeated. From John 12:24 God gave her a promise that she passionately believed and still clings to.

Verily, verily, I say unto you, Except a corn of wheat fall into the ground and die, it abideth alone: but if it die, it bringeth forth much fruit.

Without understanding why God had allowed this tragedy to come into her young life, Marianna submitted herself, without self-assertion, to God's will. The result was to be special love and honor from her peers and the fulfillment of John 12:24—Marianna was to experi-

ence one of the most celebrated careers in the history of
Bible translation.

While Mary had indeed experienced a spiritual re-
birth, she had yet to work through her doubts that the
Bible was true and that it was God's verbal revelation to
mankind. It was difficult for her to put aside the long
discussions she had had with Stannie about other world
religions. Weren't they also true? Did they not have
something to say to man? Is Christianity the only way
man can become personally related to the God of all
creation? she questioned.

But she continued to read and study her Bible daily,
and in the quietness of her own room she read about the
life, character, and teachings of Jesus Christ. As she
read, she began to see the full measure of God's love for
her. Slowly she grew in knowledge and came to understand how God wanted her to act and react in the pres-
sures of everyday life.

Her most dramatic test as a new Christian was accepting Bill's death. In him, Mary had seen a new kind of
love—a love that didn't exploit. In every way Bill had
been a true friend to her. She knew he had spoken to
her father, as well as to Marianna and Evelyn, about her
coming to the States, and he had shared the responsibility for her welfare. Now Mary, like Marianna, experienced the shattering realization that in this life Bill was
totally separated from her.

Mary was no stranger to death. She had seen many
Chol children die from disease and malnutrition. She
had seen the results of drunken machete fights. And she
had heard and seen the bitter wailing, grieving, and
abysmal lack of hope that characterized most funerals in
the Chiapas hills.

But here, on this quiet campus in the Ozark hills, Mary experienced death in a new way. It wasn't that people didn't weep—most did. They expressed sympathy for Marianna as well as disbelief and bewilderment that such a fine young man should be lost to the cause of Bible translation.

Yet there was a difference in how they accepted Bill's death. For the first time in her life, Mary glimpsed the reality, confidence, and hope that true believers in Jesus Christ possess. She understood this from the attitudes of the students and staff, and from the words Uncle Cam spoke to the sixty people attending SIL that August morning.

Just before our Lord was crucified, Jesus took a towel and some water and began to wash the disciples' feet. When He came to Peter, Peter protested and said, "Lord, You shouldn't be washing our feet." And the Lord answered Peter with these words in John 13:7: "What I do thou knowest not now; but thou shalt know hereafter."

God knows the end from the beginning. In life we see only through a dark glass. God's purposes and the way He works out His will often seem strange to us. The reason is that we don't now, nor ever will be able to, fathom God's mind and the purposes He has designed for the working out of His will in history.

This morning none of us understands why God took Bill home to be with Himself. Perhaps we will never know, on this side of eternity. But one thing is sure: God never makes a mistake, and the Lord's promise to Peter is the same promise to us. We don't know now, but some day, further on down the road of life, or when we see the Lord face to face in heaven, we'll understand why God has chosen to allow Bill to experience the joy of eternity at such an early age.

Uncle Cam's words helped. In time, Mary and others who shared this special moment came to understand that the same love that drew them into an understanding of God and His personal care for them also helped them overcome the pain of Bill's death. And this same love provided (for those who opened and submitted themselves to God's will) nourishment and strength for the hard moments that were yet to come, individually and as an organization.

Mary's hard moment was to come a few weeks later when she said good-bye to all her new friends at SIL. Apart from the shock of Bill's death (which came toward the end of SIL), that summer was uniquely happy for Mary. Her openness, enthusiasm, sense of humor, and slightly uncoordinated antics on the volleyball court made her the school darling. She had also participated in language learning classes, giving potential Bible translators language practice in soliciting information from a monolingual ethnic language helper.

And then, suddenly, it all came to an end. Mary realized that these beautiful people had become family, in some ways more important than her own family. Now they were gone. In place of her carefree happiness came a familiar melancholy and an empty loneliness.

Since many attending SIL spoke Spanish, Mary had felt little impetus (in spite of Evelyn's urging) to learn more or practice what little English she knew. Marianna and Evelyn had chosen a small Bible school for girls in Albany, New York, as the best place for Mary to get the practice she needed.

Mrs. Christie, the dean, was a godly, sensitive woman with long experience in detection of homesickness and loneliness. She understood Mary's feelings and did her best to make her feel warm and welcome. But Mrs. Christie didn't speak Spanish, and no matter how hard she tried, English words and friendly smiles did not dispel Mary's loneliness and the frustration of not being able to communicate. There was another barrier, and Mary reflected on it many years later.

In Sulphur Springs I got along well. Most of the people spoke Spanish, and they would talk to me in Spanish. Now, at this Bible school in Albany, everyone spoke English. And besides not being able to communicate, I realized all the other girls were college graduates. I felt very dumb and inferior. My background was so different from all the others.

Everyone was kind and friendly—almost too friendly. They hardly left me alone. Sometimes I wished they would because I felt like such a bother. I wanted to go away and cry.

Many of us fail to understand that God doesn't ask us about the talents we don't have. Rather, He asks us to use the love and strength and gifts we do have. In the Albany Bible School there was a teacher, Miss Jones, who was so crippled with arthritis that she literally dragged herself to class. But Miss Jones had the gift of encouragement, and she used it on Mary.

"In class I really wasn't studying anything," recalled Mary. "I went only to hear English. Yet this made no difference to Miss Jones. Whenever I was in her class she made a deliberate point to smile at me. It was the kind of smile that made me feel loved."

Encouragement is really a part of true love. The one who encourages creates opportunities for others to discover their own strengths and capabilities. It was this way for Mary. "When Miss Jones smiled at me and told

76

me I could learn English and anything else I wanted to learn, I no longer felt dumb. Miss Jones had a friend who had me in for tea two or three afternoons each week. And there, in that lovely living room, I drank tea and learned English, with words associated with actions. It was a wonderful year—quite like the joy of opening a page in an old-fashioned pop-up picture book."

And so the school year ended. Mary had turned eighteen and could speak English well enough to communicate most of her needs. But now she faced a new crisis—where to go for the summer and what to do for the next academic year. To further complicate matters, Mary's father had written her a letter strongly disapproving of her being at Albany. "I understood you would be going to a high school," wrote Stanford. "You need a high-school education and you certainly won't get this in a Bible school."

Stanford then wrote a Mr. Chaney, an old college friend who owned several manufacturing plants, and asked him to check in on Mary. Stanford even suggested that she might be given a job in one of his factories.

When Mr. Chaney met Mary and saw the Bible school, he placed his hands on his hips and said, "Your dad's crazy. This is a wonderful place for you to be. I'll write and tell him what I think of his idea of your coming to work for me. In the meantime, why don't you plan to come to our home for a weekend?"

It hurt Mary that her father didn't approve of her being at Bible school. As a dutiful daughter who dearly loved her father, she wanted to please him in every way. But she was also glad that Mr. Chaney had taken her side. She knew his words of approval for the school would carry infinitely more weight than hers. They did.

But in Stanford's mind, the problem was solved only

until the end of the school year. Then he wrote her again, suggesting she work in Mr. Chaney's factory or as a domestic in the home of another of his friends. "I think you should move out of the school as soon as possible," wrote Stanford.

Mary was again puzzled. She wanted to obey her father, yet somehow she felt his suggestions were not in keeping with what the Lord seemed to want her to do. She knew she could talk with Miss Jones about this matter. As they sipped tea and talked about the stewardship of one's life, Mary came to realize that more than anything else in the world she wanted her high-school education. And she agreed with her father about moving out of the Bible school.

While Mary had grown to love Mrs. Christie and was deeply indebted to Miss Jones, it had been a long year away from the intimacy and special warmth of her own family and home. God, who knows the deep unspoken longings of His children, provided Mary a turning point just before she had to decide whether to stay at the school all summer and pick apples or go to work for Mr. Chaney.

This turning point and crisis of choice was a part of God's plan to shape and mold Mary into His predetermined design, although she didn't realize this at the time. Divine energy acts upon the stuff of this world, as when Jesus turned water into wine. In Mary's case, God used her desire and her need for the support, affirmation, and comfort of a nuclear family to help her make the right choice at the right time.

On a motoring trip through New York State in the spring of 1942, Mr. and Mrs. Slocum decided to visit Mary at the Bible school. Observing her warmth, enthusiasm, and delightful lack of guile, they were immediately charmed. Mrs. Slocum particularly responded to and identified with Mary's fun-loving nature. She herself frequently felt and acted more like a collegian than the wife of a sophisticated engineer.

"Mary," said Mrs. Slocum, smiling, "we've been thinking. Maybe you would like to come and live with us in Ardmore. We know you don't have your high school and . . . well, there's a high school directly across the street from our home and you could live with us and go to . . ."

Instantly, a joy began to well up inside of Mary. It drowned out Mrs. Slocum's words—words about how much she and Mr. Slocum would enjoy having her, about the room on the third floor Mary could have as her own, about the fine young people at their Tenth Presbyterian Church in Philadelphia.

These were words from out of a dream, and it was all Mary could do to keep from exploding. She wanted to scream, "I can't believe what you are asking me! Do you know how I have longed to be in a home? To have a room of my own, where I can be alone to cry when I feel lonely?"

Mary didn't scream or shout out her deep feelings. But she did wiggle with anticipation, and she told the Slocums how happy she was they were asking her. She also told them about her father's suggestion. "We quite understand your situation," said Mrs. Slocum. "Why don't we stay overnight in Albany. This will give you time to think about whether you would like to come with us, or go to live with your father's friend."

Even before the Slocums left the school that morning, Mary knew she would go with them. And when the Slocums returned the following morning for Mary's answer, she ran into their outstretched arms. From that moment, and for eight happy years, Mary became another daughter in the Slocum household.

For five of those eight years, Mary pursued an exhaustive, nonstop leapfrog school schedule. Since she had completed sixth grade in Mexico, the Ardmore school system placed Mary in a seventh-grade summer school program. "It will perfect her English and she will be ready for the eighth grade in September," said the school counselor. And Mary was. But she was also nineteen.

Her age, not the fact that she was taller than her thirteen- and fourteen-year-old classmates, began to bother Mary. But then the feeling she had when she left the *Alianza*—that she was destined for something more than what she had experienced or known on the coffee plantation—flooded her thinking.

"I knew the poor and uneducated of Mexico had no chance to be anything other than what their fathers and their fathers before had been," said Mary, reflecting on her early schooling in Philadelphia.* "I was experiencing a great opportunity and was grateful to God and the Slocums for their love and practical help. So it didn't matter that I was older than my classmates. Besides, no one laughed or made fun. In fact, all the kids liked the idea of having me in class, and they helped me when they could. The teachers were also kind and patient with me. They always told me to come back after school if I needed help to understand something—and I usually did!"

After eighth grade, Mary took her freshman year

---

*This statement reflects the general attitude prevalent in rural Mexico in the thirties and forties. Currently, wide-range government school programs have done much to change this attitude.

during the summer and began her sophomore year in the fall. The routine was hard but going well, so well that Mary enrolled in twice-weekly classes at the Pennsylvania Bible Institute. Her big ambition was to graduate from high school and Bible school at the same time, and she did!

She undertook this double load not because she felt herself particularly studious, nor because she attacked her projects with tremendous enthusiasm; rather, she did it for her father.

At the end of her junior year, Stanford, on a business trip to Connecticut, suffered a paralyzing stroke and was hospitalized. In order to be near her father, Mary went to Connecticut and took a job in the hospital laundry room. There, during the long, hot summer, Mary spent her free time with her father—praying, reading passages of Scripture, and explaining why she had come to faith in Jesus Christ.

Mary also tried to explain why her mother had professed faith in Jesus Christ. (Evelyn, who had continued to work with the Chols, had written Mary that Elodia had publicly confessed her faith and was attending the church in Tumbalá. "It was a courageous step," said Evelyn, "and marked a turning point in her life that had taken several years of questioning before she slowly came to understand her spiritual need.")

After several weeks in the hospital, Stanford rallied and insisted he be flown back to Mexico. "If I am going to die, I want to die in my own home, in my own bed," he said. Stannie, who had seen active military duty in North Africa and Italy, was mustered out after he was wounded, and he also came to Connecticut. When his father insisted on returning, Stannie had no alternative but to spend what little money the family had and fly his father back to what was now a humble cottage in Yajalón.

"Father," said Mary, "I want to go back with you. I am stronger than Mother and can take better care of you."

"No," said Stanford weakly, "your schooling—you have worked hard. You must stay and finish. You will make me happier by getting your diploma."

Now more determined than ever, Mary returned to Ardmore and a full study load. Then one day near Christmas time, Mary was hurrying home with a big bag of groceries in her arms. Suddenly, she slipped and fell on a patch of ice. The groceries scattered everywhere, and for some reason Mary couldn't get up.

Mrs. Slocum was out visiting her sister, and Mr. Slocum, who was hard of hearing, was in his attic study. Mary knew he couldn't hear her if she called for help, and as she lay there she wondered what would happen to her. Then she heard a gentle voice ask, "Are you all right?"

It was an older woman who had driven by and had seen Mary lying on the sidewalk. Mary told her what had happened, and the lady called to two workmen down the street, who came and lifted Mary into the house. As they carried her inside, one of the men accidentally knocked her foot. Then Mary knew why she hadn't been able to get up; she had a broken leg!

She began a long, painful convalescence which was complicated by a cast that was molded too tight and by bones that refused to knit. Remarkably, Mary kept up her high school work with the help of teachers and students who brought in work. Mr. Slocum proved a remarkable algebra tutor.

And when the snow melted and the time came for the

June graduation exercises, Mary proudly hobbled up
the steps of the platform to receive her high school diploma. She was twenty-three.

Happy and relieved to have reached and passed this
important milestone in her life, her graduation day was
marked both with joy and ambivalence. It was a joyful
time because as a graduation gift Marianna surprised
Mary by sending her sister Margarita to the graduation
ceremonies. It was the first time in five years that Mary
had seen her younger sister. As she had done with
Mary, Marianna persuaded the Morisons to allow Margarita to come to the United States for an education.
And like Mary, she was to live in the Slocum household.

Mary's ambivalence was due to her inner struggle.
What was she going to do with her life now? While living
with the Slocums, she had attended the Tenth Presbyterian Church in Philadelphia. Through the powerful
preaching of its pastor, Dr. Donald Grey Barnhouse,
Mary had come to understand that the church had a
responsibility for worldwide cross-cultural missions.
Mary agreed with her pastor and with those who came
for special missions conferences that there was a need
for cross-cultural Christian workers—that is, as long as
they didn't expect *her* to respond to this need.

"When I went to missions conferences," recalled
Mary, "I learned I had a responsibility to share with
others what I had learned about Jesus Christ. But I
didn't want to do my sharing in any jungle. I knew what
it was like to live in isolation. I was willing to share my
faith with others in the city, perhaps as a secretary,
which is what I wanted to become."

Yet Mary, who still had much to learn about God and
how He leads, had learned early in her Christian life
that if she acknowledged Jesus Christ as Lord, He was

exactly that. And to live at peace with herself and with Him, she had to obey the inner promptings of her soul. Thus she went to Wycliffe's SIL course for the summer of 1946.

Mary's memory of SIL was the SIL of five years before, when she had been the darling of the school, and where the staff and students felt like one big family. But in 1946 it was different. The institute was larger and more sophisticated, and for the first time Mary was introduced to the science of descriptive linguistics. It was an alien world of syntax, morphology, phonetics, glottal stops, and bilabial fricatives. "I made just a passing grade, and I would have to confess it wasn't my most enjoyable summer," said Mary.

Mary's attention to her studies was disturbed by the constant gnawing feeling that since her father was ill, she should be by his side to help her mother. Just before her final exams, and before she knew if she had been accepted as a Wycliffe worker, Mary did what she felt she must.

"I feel the Lord led me here to SIL," Mary told SIL director Dr. Richard Pittman. "I also feel the Lord is calling me to the mission field, but I don't know when it will be. Right now my father is sick and I think my place is with him, to help my mother take care of him." Dr. Pittman, a sensitive man, agreed, and Mary left immediately for Mexico and her first reunion with her family in five years.

If the summer of 1946 was cheerless for Mary, it was brimming with joy and happiness for Evelyn. There at SIL, among the students who, like Mary, were trying to make sense out of the new and strange linguistic vocabulary, was a man named Wilbur Aulie. While Evelyn explained these new terms to the students, Wilbur, a twenty-nine-year-old accountant from Chicago, hung on her every word.

As it is with the way of a man and a maid, they fell in love. They were engaged before the SIL course ended, and married in September. Evelyn returned with her new husband to work and live in Tumbalá among the Chol people.

This sudden turn of events pleased Mary. She was happy for the friendship of Evelyn and Wilbur, and appreciated their prayerful support. Like Bill Bentley, Wilbur became a friend to the Morison household, especially to Stanford.

On one occasion, several months after he had been in Tumbalá, Wilbur visited Stanford on his sickbed. Just before Wilbur was about to leave, he read from Romans 8. When he came to verse 33, he explained that anyone who placed his faith and trust in God's Son, Jesus Christ, would on the promise of Almighty God be acquitted from all sin and never be condemned. Wilbur then brought Stanford's attention to verse 35.

> Who shall separate us from the love of Christ? shall tribulation, or distress, or persecution, or famine, or nakedness, or peril, or sword?

Wilbur was about to continue reading and explaining the passage when Stanford asked, in a quiet, reflective mood, "That word *separation*; what does it mean?"

Wilbur used Stanford's question as a springboard to explain what separation meant to those who lived their lives independently of God's will and purposes.

Wilbur concluded and was about to leave, when Stanford said softly, "The hymns my daughter Mary sings to me, the words she reads from her Bible—I believe them."

"I'm glad you do," said Wilbur quietly. He then said good-bye and left. It was the last time Wilbur saw Stanford alive. At the hands of an irresponsible doctor (his regular doctor was out of town), Stanford suffered a tragic reaction to a blood transfusion and within fifteen minutes he went into shock and respiratory collapse. He died gasping and choking.

For several weeks after her father's death, Mary experienced a sense of disorientation and inability to make future plans. It had been just a year since she had left SIL, but it had been twelve intense months, with little for Mary to think about except her father's comfort. With his death her responsibility was over. Stannie had assumed responsibility for their mother and inherited what was left of their father's business.

Now Mary was free to pursue what she felt was her unfinished education. But the problem was where and what to study, and how to pay for it. Her one big dream—to become a secretary and live in a big city in her own apartment—changed to a desire for a nursing career. But if a miracle didn't happen, Mary knew her expectation would indeed be only a dream.

Just when she began to think there were no alternatives but to remain in Yajalón, Mary received a letter from the Slocums.

"I can't believe it!" Mary said to her mother. "The Slocums want me to come and live with them again and go to school."

"But you have your high school diploma," reminded Elodia.

"I know, I know," said Mary excitedly. "And that's the reason they're writing me. They say someone has provided a scholarship for me to study nursing at Presbyterian Hospital in Philadelphia. The Slocums want me to come right away."

CHAPTER SIX

How Will You Know Me
If You Don't Marry Me?

A few weeks before Mary had left for her year in Mexico
to care for her father, a quiet, intelligent Norwegian
with a shock of red hair and a Ph.D. after his name
asked if he might write her. He was kind and con-
siderate, and there was an easy rapport in their friendship. Frankly, Mary was astonished that Gunnar felt
warm toward her when she felt he was so far "above"
her. He had even hinted that while she was in Mexico he
might be able to come and visit her.

But the more Gunnar showed his affection for her,
the more she felt threatened—threatened that he would
become "too serious" and that her life goals for an education might be thwarted. Not really understanding why
she said it, Mary told him, "No. It wouldn't be wise for
you to come. I like you, but I've got to finish my schooling." Gunnar seemed to understand. He honored
Mary's request, and walked out of her life.

But it hadn't been as easy for Mary. While in Mexico attending to her father, she occasionally had wondered if it was worth sacrificing Gunnar for a higher education. And when she began her training at Presbyterian Hospital in Philadelphia and saw men who reminded her of him, she felt a jab of loneliness inside. For that moment the world seemed without warmth or comfort—but then Mary's quick mind would again be fully absorbed in what she was doing.

Nursing became her life, except for one blind date that literally ended up a flop. It had been an ice-skating date, and Mary had spent most of the evening slipping, sliding, and collapsing on the ice. It was her only date until the summer of 1952.

But before that summer, Mary received a request from Marianna to come to the Tzeltal village of Corralito and work as her temporary partner. (Marianna's permanent partner—Florence Gerdel, a registered nurse—was home in the United States for an extended leave.) Mary's response was short: "I'll come. I feel it's what God would have me do." But behind that short, simple statement of commitment were long, agonizing hours of inner debate and deliberation.

First there was the obstacle of how Mary perceived herself. Her peers, then and now, regard her highly both as a person and for her professional skills and insight. But in some deep recess of her being, a lying, gnawing voice told her she was inadequate, that she wasn't trained well enough to handle the emergencies peculiar to a remote jungle clinic. Marianna had written of the wonderful way the Lord was working among the Tzeltals; about the more than one thousand believers and the little clinic that handled about seventy outpatients a day. And although Mary truly rejoiced with

Marianna over the way God was working, the success stories served only to reinforce her fears.

Then there was Mary's mother. Elodia was more than a little proud of her daughter, who now had her own apartment, was making her first money working as a private nurse, and who had a group of wholesome friends. No more of the hard, lonely demanding life in the Chiapas highlands for her daughter, Elodia thought.

Mary knew her mother felt this way, and imagined she would feel Mary was going to Corralito out of a sense of indebtedness. How could she explain to her mother that never once in all the years she had lived with the Slocums had they said one word or even hinted she should pay them back for giving her an education?

Further, there had never been the slightest suggestion that Mary return to Mexico as a missionary nurse. Whenever Mary had spoken to the Slocums about cross-cultural service, they wisely urged her to seek God's guidance and do what He indicated, not what others thought she should do.

Mary was also coming to grips with her own value system. The year Mary spent with her father and the year she lived in her own apartment taught her important lessons.

"When I was nursing and had worked all day and came home to my apartment, I often asked myself what I was really doing," said Mary. "The longer I worked, the more I realized I was working just to pay bills. There didn't seem to be any meaning to my life and work.

"As I thought about life, it came to me that materialism destroys when it becomes all a person thinks about. My father died poor—everything he had worked for was gone. As I reflected on this, I saw that the most important things in life are not money, or power, or importance, or property. In the end, the important thing is love—Christian love. All my father's money and property were gone, but he had his family—people who loved him—and when you're dying this is all that matters.

"All these thoughts came into my mind as I considered Marianna's letter and service with Wycliffe Bible Translators. And the more I thought, the more I decided my goals were not going to be a big house or lots of money. My goal was going to be people, loving them and serving them any way I could."

While Mary didn't want to make money her main pursuit in life, she still needed money to sustain herself on the field. Like all Wycliffe workers, Mary was responsible for raising her own support. When the Tenth Presbyterian Church learned of Mary's intentions to join Wycliffe and work with the Tzeltals in southern Mexico, they said they would pray for her. Mary was grateful for their support in prayer, but this did not take the place of financial support.

Then one day Mrs. Slocum phoned Mary while she was at work. "Mary, I called to tell you that some mail came for you, and one letter from the Wycliffe office looks important. Do you want me to open it?"

"Yes! Yes, open it!" urged Mary.

"Oh, Mary," exclaimed Mrs. Slocum. "You won't believe this. You have received your whole support. Someone has promised to send in a hundred dollars each month."

"Who is the person?" asked Mary.

"I don't know," said Mrs. Slocum. "It's anonymous. But I don't want you to think we're the ones who are giving this to you. We're not. God truly has set His seal of approval on your endeavor by giving you the money you need."

For the next five years, Mary's supporter faithfully sent one hundred dollars each month. Her anonymous donor finally revealed herself as the now Mrs. Kathy Kroeges. Mary had known Kathy before and met her again during a missions conference at Urbana, Illinois, and in a passing conversation Mary mentioned she intended to go to Mexico.

"Are you ready to go?" Kathy had asked.

"The only thing I don't have is my support," Mary had confided, and that was that.

Two months later, Mary received news of the anonymous gift.

Early in her Christian experience, and quite apart from self-interest, Mary demonstrated that she possessed the courage to combine her love for people with her love for God. And during her work among the Tzeltals, this embryo of courage and love, like all things great in character, grew slowly until it became a normal, demonstrable part of her lifestyle. In fact, it grew to be such a part of her that she herself was, and is to this present day, not fully aware of her lovely gift.

But Marianna was not unaware of Mary's unique spiritual talent. Out of her keen perception she wrote her parents how happy she was to have Mary as part of the Tzeltal team.

> When I think back and remember Mary's indifference at seventeen and see how energetic she is for the Lord and the Tzeltal people, I am overcome with joy and gratitude to God.
>
> Besides being a tremendous help in the primitive situation in which we live here in Corralito, Mary is just lots of fun to be with. She is also most resourceful. One day a

whole column of soldiers showed up unexpectedly for lunch. I hardly knew what to do, but from the years of experience on her father's ranch of providing meals for people who dropped in unexpectedly, Mary took over and made our small rations go a long way.

Mary also cares for the sick and dying who come to our clinic with such love and understanding compassion that many have been drawn to the Lord through her. Since she learned to speak Chol in her childhood from the workers who lived and worked on her father's coffee ranch, Mary has learned to speak the related Tzeltal language quickly and uses it in her medical work.

As I watch Mary work, I am often amused by the way she calls all the backwoods Indian women "ladies."

"Here is a lady with a very sick child," she says, and then proceeds to treat them with all the care, tenderness, and proper courtesy of a sophisticated educated woman.

Some of Mary's favorite patients are the calloused witch doctors of the area, and they, like all of us, have fallen under her spell of tenderness and caring.

There have been many events that have happened to Mary during her time with me and the Tzeltals, but I remember one day that stands out above all the rest.

Early one morning, Tomás, a young Tzeltal Christian, came to our clinic carrying his wife in a chair strapped to his back. Mary and another nurse, Marj Truline, also here temporarily, examined the woman and found she was dying in abnormal childbirth. Quickly Mary assisted and helped Marj improvise an operating table in a thatched hut, and with prayer and the skill of her training Marj was able to save the life of the young woman with an emergency operation.

While Marianna considered the saving of this young woman's life a major achievement, Mary hardly remembers the event. What she does remember is the summer of 1952. She returned to Sulphur Springs and took part in an orientation course for new members. As is frequently the case in missions organizations, there were more single women than single men—a ratio of eight to three that summer. According to a survey of discriminating maidens of the class of '52, a tall, dark, quiet-spoken native of Arkansas—Orville Johnson—was, in their opinion, the best of the lot.

"Hey," said a friend to Mary one afternoon, "there's Johnson. Don't you think he's cute?"

"How can you tell?" said Mary. "All I can see is the back of his head."

"Believe me, he's a honey," said another friend. "And we've all set out to catch him. What about you, Mary? Are you going to try?"

"No, not me," said Mary in mock seriousness. "I have someone else in mind. Besides, I don't think I'll ever get married. Men like him don't notice girls like me."

But Mary was wrong. Orv Johnson had indeed noticed the vivacious Mary Morison several nights before at a party. Orv had a reputation as a rugged outdoors man. On the court he could spike one of the meanest volleyballs, and he seemed comfortable just to be with "the boys." But he was quietly looking for a life partner. He was also looking for the right opportunity to approach this vibrant woman.

In passing conversation with Mary one day, Orv learned how much she enjoyed the casual warmth of a home and family.

"Well, I live with my mother a short distance from Sulphur Springs," said Orv. "If you like good home cooking, I'd be happy to take you home for dinner."

It was Mary's first date with Orv, and it brought raised eyebrows and knowing "ahas" from her girlfriends.

"It doesn't mean a thing," Mary assured them.

"That's what you think," warned her friends. "A boy doesn't take a girl home to meet his mother for nothing!"

The second date came a dozen days later, when Harriet Swauger, an observer to this budding romance and a self-proclaimed matchmaker, decided Orv needed some prodding. Harriet asked Orv one day if he would like to drive Mary and her to a nearby community.

"My husband's out of town and I don't drive. It would be a great favor. Besides, it will be fun for Mary and me to get out for a drive."

Orv took the bait. But there was more to Harriet's plan.

"We've had a great time, Orv," said Harriet, when they got back. "It's late, and it's a long drive back over narrow winding roads. There's a spare bedroom, and in the morning Mary can fix pancakes for you."

The plot had all the subtleness of a herd of stampeding elephants—but it worked. "Thank you," said Orv. "That's a good idea. I'll stay the night."

The conversation over breakfast the next morning was filled with pleasant trivia, and the pancakes were done to a "T."

A few days later, Mary left Sulphur Springs to resume her duties at the Corralito Clinic. Before she left, Harriet asked if anything had come of her little strategy. "I guess not," said Mary. "He just said good-bye."

"But he's going to take his jungle training in Mexico this fall," said Harriet, "and he'll practically be next door to you at Corralito."

"I won't be able to see him there," said Mary. "There won't be time for either of us to get away. Besides, I don't think he's really interested in me, and that's okay by me."

"I'm not so sure he isn't interested in you," said Harriet. "If he's the one for you, God will find a way to bring you both together."

In preparation for pioneer work with Wycliffe, all beginning members must spend three months at a jungle boot camp—"Jungle Camp," as it's known in Wycliffe circles.

The training at Jungle Camp emphasized an array of practical skills—like swimming; skulling through white-water rapids; and constructing a hut, a mud stove, and furniture out of jungle cane, using only jungle vines to tie it all together. Included too were courses in tropical medicine, language learning, jungle survival techniques, axmanship, and many other skills a pioneer Bible translator might need.

For Orv, much of this was child's play. After all, he had grown up on a small farm and had learned to handle an ax before the age most children learn to use crayons. It was, therefore, all the more painful when one day Orv had to go to the Jungle Camp infirmary to have his split toe stitched up. He had stayed on after his Jungle Camp training, and his ax had accidentally careened off a log he was chopping and hit his toe.

To further dampen Orv's spirits, he hadn't heard from Mary. Shortly after his arrival at Jungle Camp's Main Base, Orv had written Mary a short note. He knew Corralito was just minutes away via Missionary Aviation Fellowship (MAF), and it was on MAF's regularly scheduled stops to and from Jungle Camp. But the pilot had forgotten to deliver Orv's letter.

In the meantime, Mary, after four months of treating

people from early morning to late afternoon, decided to take a two-week break at Jungle Camp's Main Base. Still embarrassed that such an accident could happen to him, Orv used his homemade crutches to hobble down to the airstrip that mid-morning in November. He was never the same again.

With a dimpled smile and her good-natured charm fizzing like sparkling water, Mary slipped out of that MAF Piper and into Orv's waiting heart. These two people, who had walked alone all their lives, seldom letting others know their deep feelings, spent long, lazy days together, sensing an underlying closeness when they looked deep into one another's eyes.

There had been little "romance" in Orv's life. His father had died in Orv's early boyhood, and he had seen the hard reality of his own family and others desperately struggling to survive during the Great Depression. Orv had seen families draw on energies that went beyond the popular notion of romance and courtship.

Oh, he didn't deny the feeling of being off balance, of his hands turning cold and sweaty whenever he was near Mary, but he wasn't one given to convention and decorum. He proposed in the most natural way he knew.

"I'm pretty sure I'll be assigned to Peru," he said as he tied a heavy cedar canoe by the river bank. "How about coming with me?"

"Peru?" repeated Mary. "I'm not ready to go to Peru. I've heard it's always misty and cold in Lima. Besides, I don't know you well enough."

"But," countered Orv with a wide smile, "how will you ever get to know me if you don't marry me?"

Orv's proposal was simple and straightforward, but Mary's response was neither yes nor no, and Orv decided not to press the matter. Just before Mary left to return to Corralito, Orv asked if she was going to attend the 1953 biennial conference at Sulphur Springs in September.

"No, I don't think so," said Mary. "Not too many people are interested in my opinions." But Mary was wrong. In a letter from her director, Dr. George Cowan, she learned that she was expected to attend the conference, if at all possible.

The setting for Wycliffe's biennial conference at Sulphur Springs looked like an old-fashioned country fair. The buildings were white-sided, with open beam ceilings and large screens in place of windows. There were few sidewalks, just coarse pasture grass and gravel driveways. But the moon there looked every bit as silvery and compelling as it had in the Chiapas Jungle Camp.

One evening after the business meeting and reports, Orv decided it was again time to press his question of marriage.

"You know that field assignments are often changed," said Orv in a casual tone. "I have been assigned to Ecuador instead of Peru."

"Oh, you're going to Ecuador?" said Mary. "Then I'll go with you." And for the first time, Orv reached over and kissed his bride-to-be. Up until this moment they hadn't even held hands, which was not surprising for a proper Mexican girl. Although Mary had an American father, her roots of decorum and respectability were deeply Latin.

To announce this most momentous step, Orv wrote a letter to his friends. The letter was dated December, 1953.

Greetings from Mexico. I arrived here December 17, but before getting into Mexico I had to get a visa. At the Mexican Consulate, one of the officials asked me why I was going to Mexico. "To get married," I said. . . .

Let me tell you a little about her. Her name is Mary Morison. She attended Philadelphia Bible Institute, is a registered nurse, and for the past two years has worked among the Tzeltal people of southern Mexico.

We will be married December 30 in Mexico City. Then, as soon as possible, we will go to Ecuador. Remember Mary and me as we prepare to translate God's Word for a group of people who have never heard of God's wonderful gift—His Son Jesus Christ.

The wedding was all that weddings are supposed to be—a proper white gown, a stone church, and a big pre-wedding dinner given by Mary's favorite brother Stannie. Longtime friends came to congratulate the couple.

There were even some nervous second thoughts.

"You know," Mary said to Orv the day before the wedding, "you've never told me you love me. And here we are going to be married tomorrow, and I'm not sure about this."

During the years before Orv had placed his faith in Jesus Christ, he had seen men tell women they loved them in order to get sex. And the women, wanting love, gave in.

The feelings Orv had for Mary were quite beyond the power of his shy vocabulary. When he told her he "liked" her, he was in effect telling her that his feelings for her went beyond the word "love," which for him held connotations of lust.

Mary, on the other hand, wanted some reassurance that what she was about to do was right. Orv, in his

100

positive, forward-looking attitude (an attitude that Mary now thanks God for) said, "That's okay, Mary, if you're not sure—because I am!"

The next day, no one would have guessed Mary had ever expressed such doubts. When she walked down the aisle and out of the church on Orv's strong arm as Mrs. Johnson, it seemed there was no doubt that Orv was the man God had chosen for her.

Marianna, acting as Mary's maid of honor and looking as pretty as the bride, declared she had never seen a more beautiful bride or a happier groom.

Marianna was right; Orv was indeed happy. But his bliss quickly turned to bewilderment when Mary expressed a strong desire to spend an extended time with her immediate family. After all, most of the weddings she had seen as a young girl on her father's ranch had lasted at least three days. Here was Orv urging her to leave almost immediately after the reception.

In the end, Orv's will prevailed and the newlyweds spent a three-day honeymoon in Acapulco. There Orv began to learn about the idiosyncrasies of his new wife, such as her passion to move furniture. No room, it seemed, was quite comfortable to Mary until she had rearranged at least a chair or a table.

But after all, idiosyncrasies are what make each person and couple unique, interesting, and special. And their "specialness" would endear Orv and Mary to their colleagues and to the people God had chosen for them to love—the Secoya people of Ecuador, South America.

CHAPTER SEVEN

Never Touch a Tiger

With feelings born out of his intimate encounter with the diverse character of the Republic of Ecuador, Victor W. Von Hagen, explorer and archeological historian wrote the following: "The dominate factor in Ecuador, as in all Andean republics, is its mountains. They divide the country and separate its people."

Von Hagen further noted that while the Andes run down the entire length of Ecuador from Colombia to Peru, they are "unlike the Andes in Peru whose big ranges are like horses in a troika." "Rather," he said, "Ecuador's Andes are reduced to two main ranges called the eastern and western cordillera when there is only a sprinkling of peoples, Indians of variegated tribes."*

To the east of the territory described by Von Hagen

*Victor W. Von Hagen, *Ecuador* (Caracas: Plata Publishing, Ltd, 1975), p. 8. 1975), p. 8.

begins the vast upper Amazon Basin. And here also are only a "sprinkling of peoples." One of these tiny dots drew Orv and Mary's attention—the Secoya people, a small group who lived in clusters of fifty to sixty people in the upper Ecuadorian Amazon basin, a territory on the eastern side of the massive Andes—the Ecuadorians simply call it the *Oriente* (east).

In a country a little larger than Colorado, the thickly forested, silent, often deadly *Oriente* comprises a third of Ecuador's land mass. Yet it boasts no snow-capped mountains like the ones that stand as giant sentinels about Quito, Ecuador's nine-thousand-foot-high capital. Rather, the *Oriente* has trees—over six hundred species, including the balsa, the rubber, and the famous *cinchona* from which the world gets its quinine.

Spawned also from that humid earth are insects of a variety that defy description—insects like termites, black ants, mosquitoes, june bugs, stingless bees, and more.

There are also more than 400 different kinds of birds, plus dozens of different butterflies. There are animals like the tapir, wild pig, monkey, and jaguar. There is also an abundance of fish. Some, like one species of catfish, have mouths large enough to swallow a small child.

And of course, there are the reptiles—the dreaded snakes that come out of nowhere and almost always kill. They not only kill animals, they also kill people. In the *Oriente,* animals and insects and reptiles share the same space with five different ethnic peoples.*

In January, 1956, the name of one of these ethnic minorities became a household word when five young American missionaries were speared to death on a re-

---

*WBT/SIL is currently at work with eight different ethnic minorities throughout Educador.

mote jungle river sandbar. Overnight, the name *Auca* became synonymous with savage killer.*

But there are other ethnic minorities like the Cayapa and Cofan who are virtually unknown to the rest of the world. Some people know about the interesting Colorado and Jivaro (now called Shuar) peoples. Many more know about the large number of Quichuas, but almost no one knows about the Secoyas. All that Mary and Orv knew about them in 1954 was that they were a small group of only a few hundred people who lived in northeastern Ecuador.

And how could they know more? The Secoyas lived in isolation and spoke a language (unwritten) totally different from Spanish, Ecuador's national language.

After waiting a year in Quito and Wycliffe's jungle center on the Llushin River (the Limon Cocha base began in 1957), Orv and Mary and their firstborn son, Omar, were given permission by a local chief to live among the Secoyas. On an earlier survey trip into Secoya territory, Orv and a JAARS** pilot, Omer Bondurant, had observed a Secoya area near a large oxbow lake.

"If you can get permission to settle by that lake down there," said Omer as they banked to land, "it will be a perfect spot for me to service."

"Suits me fine," said Orv. "What's the lake called?"

"Cuyabeno," Omer answered.

There were no drum tattoos or silver trumpets to mark that September day in 1955 when the little party stepped off the float plane onto the bank of Lake Cuyabeno. There should have been. They were royalty

*For a complete account of the way God worked among the Aucas, see *The Dayuma Story* by Ethel Wallis (Harper & Row, 1960). Also *Aucas Downriver* by Ethel Wallis (Harper & Row, 1973).

**Jungle Aviation and Radio Service.

at its finest—servants of the most high King! But they were also children of this high King by reason of their personal faith in Jesus Christ. And they had come to this remote lakeside to share what they themselves had heard and seen and felt.

Although Orv and Mary were thinking more of earthly things—like not slipping in the mud, and how to change baby Omar's diaper while keeping him out of reach of the mosquitos—this historic moment calls to mind Blaise Pascal's famous dictum:

> Not only do we know God by Christ alone, but we know ourselves only by Jesus Christ. Apart from Him, we do not know what is our life, nor our death, nor God, nor ourselves.
>
> Thus, without the Scripture, which has Jesus Christ alone for its object, we know nothing. We see only darkness and confusion in the nature of God and in our own nature.

This indeed was the reality of why they were there, and why each Wycliffe translator does what he does. But Mary had no such thoughts of grandeur. Many years later she wrote about how she felt at that moment:

> I remember my first impression when we landed at the lake that day. It was frightening. Three large Secoya families had come to watch us. They all stood on the bank silently, faces painted with red achiote dye, knives in their hands. As the plane floated to shore, I felt each pair of eyes fixed on me. It was obvious they had never, or hardly ever, seen a white woman with such a white baby. They just stared and stared at us. I looked at them and tried to smile. I felt so very unfit for the job I believed God had called us to do.

And so Orv and Mary began their work. Their mandate was straightforward: learn and analyze the Secoya language and culture, translate the New Testament into the Secoya language, minister to their physical needs, and while making friends, pray for God to break through to their spiritual consciousness, so that the Good News of His love might be comprehensible to their hearts and minds.

Orv knew that before he could understand the subtleties of Secoya culture, he had to know what was important to them, what they feared, and why. Sometimes the discovery of these cultural phenomena was more serious than Orv or Mary could have imagined.

Late one afternoon, about three months after he and Mary arrived in the village they now called Cuyabeno, Orv and his language helper Cesario were working intently on a particular Secoya speech pattern. In the three months Orv and Mary had been in Cuyabeno, they had learned enough of the Secoya language to greet people, carry on a limited conversation in the present tense, and learn the names of certain plants, trees, insects, animals, and household objects.

At about five in the afternoon, Gabriel, another indian, ran up to the Johnsons' hut. All Orv could pick out of the man's excited, rapid speech was the word "tigre."* Not fully understanding, Orv laughed nervously, wondering if the man was joking. But there was no mirth in Cesario's eyes, and Orv realized that the man was serious: He had seen a jaguar at the edge of the village.

It was logical that the man should come to Orv for

*Tigre, Spanish for "tiger," is a generic word used by many people in Latin America in reference to jaguars and other jungle cats.

help. He was, after all, the only one in the village with a gun that wasn't tied together, rusted, or subject to misfiring.

Orv was a hunter, a natural outdoors man from the hills of Arkansas. At the age of nine he had received his first single-shot twenty-two rifle. And like hundreds of other American boys who grew up during the Great Depression, Orv had helped to supplement his family's diet by shooting rabbits. So his natural hunting instincts immediately came alive.

Grabbing a half-dozen double zero shells and his 12-gauge Winchester pump, Orv called to Mary that he and Gabriel were off to track down a jaguar. They walked single file to the riverbank, and from there about a half mile downstream to Gabriel's hut. There they climbed into a canoe and paddled downstream about one hundred yards.

Then Orv heard it—the unmistakable, deep roar of a jaguar. No one spoke, but Gabriel looked at Orv and nodded his head. Orv got the "I-told-you-so" message and needed no further convincing. He quickly pumped a shell into the chamber of his Winchester as Gabriel guided the canoe to the riverbank and steadied it by holding onto the long, overhanging grass.

Gabriel motioned for Orv to stay in the canoe. To Orv's surprise, he began to make jaguar-like noises. Orv wasn't sure how long Gabriel expected him to sit there, so he began to move. But once again the man motioned for him to wait, and he continued his jaguar noises, punctuated with periods of silence.

After half an hour had passed, Orv said, "He's gone." But Gabriel was not so sure, and he paddled about fifteen yards downstream and waited some more. It was beginning to get dark, and Orv was about to say again he was sure the jaguar was long gone.

Suddenly, there was a rustling in the dry leaves. Almost before Orv had time to think, the jaguar came into view on the riverbank above them, about twenty-five yards from where they sat in the canoe. Orv aimed and fired. There was a terrible roar and thrashing about.

"Shoot him again!" Gabriel cried. "Shoot him again! He's up, he's up!"

But Orv couldn't shoot again. The flash from the gun had momentarily blinded him. Orv tried to give the gun to Gabriel but he wouldn't take it. There was only one thing to do. With his night vision clearing a little, Orv pointed the gun in the direction Gabriel indicated and pulled the trigger.

There was a roar, but not from the jaguar. It was Gabriel's victory yell. Then from upstream came another noise. The Secoyas who had been awaiting the outcome of this great hunt began to beat the sides of their canoes with their paddles.

Mary, of course, had no way of knowing what was happening, and when she heard the pounding of the canoes she feared the worst.

Orv, realizing he had killed the jaguar, climbed out of the canoe to examine what the Secoyas called *tigre*. The jaguar's skin was too beautiful to rot in the jungle, so he asked Gabriel to help him get the dead animal into the canoe. He refused.

"How strange," thought Orv, as he grabbed the cat's tail and dragged the one hundred and fifty-pound dead weight to the river's edge while Gabriel stood and watched in silence.

"At least someone will help me get it out of the canoe

when we get back to the village," he thought. But he was mistaken. Although every Secoya in the village turned out to watch his return, no one would help him.

It was then that Orv knew something was wrong. No one would shake his hand, and the children who usually played around their home were nowhere to be seen. He had become an untouchable—an outcast—but why? Puzzled by this unexpected turn of events, Orv fell asleep to the buzz of jungle crickets and the taunts of Satan telling him his effectiveness in Cuyabeno was over before it had begun.

The following morning, on a routine "house" call to attend Matilde, the mother of a sickly four-day-old baby, Mary discovered why Orv was being ostracized.

"*Doña* Maria, everyone in the village says my baby Elias is going to die."

"Why do they all say this?" asked Mary.

"Because your husband touched the tiger."

"Touched the tiger? I don't understand."

"Yes, the shaman and all the elders say it is wrong to touch a tiger when there is a newborn child in the village."

Later, as Mary explained to Orv what she had discovered, both came to the startling realization that their future effectiveness among the Secoyas depended upon whether this four-day-old baby lived or died. And from Mary's prognosis, it seemed that the child would die.

CHAPTER EIGHT

The Testing

Touching the dead jaguar was a normal and natural action for a hunter. But if Orv had understood the Secoyas' preoccupation with the spirit world, he surely would have acted differently.

He had become an outcast because according to Secoya tribal teaching, this newborn child would get dysentery and die because Orv hadn't observed the correct prohibition after killing a jaguar.

When Mary first discovered why the Secoyas were treating Orv as an outcast, she and Orv made the problem a matter of earnest prayer. "Lord," they prayed, "if You want us to remain here and translate Your Word for these people, then please keep the child alive. We know You are the only One who can perform this miracle."

About three weeks after the jaguar incident, God not

only answered their prayer but allowed Mary to be part of the answer. Matilde, the mother of the newborn child, came to Mary one morning complaining of a bad cold. "My baby Elias is hot, too," she said. Mary gave Matilde some medicine, then examined Elias's lungs with her stethoscope. "Your baby has a severe case of pneumonia," Mary told Matilde. After giving Elias a penicillin injection and instructing Matilde how to care for her son, mother and child left.

Hardly five minutes had passed when Matilde reappeared with Elias in her outstretched arms. "I brought my baby to you alive, and now he is dying." Mary took one look at Elias's blue, contorted face, and she knew he was choking to death.

Without a word of explanation, Mary grabbed Elias, turned him upside down, and slapped him firmly on his back. Immediately his throat cleared of the obstruction. He gave a cry and began to breathe normally. And Mary, with a deep sense of relief and gratitude to God, handed Elias back to his mother.

That Matilde should return to Mary for help at just the right moment was all the evidence Mary and Orv needed to thank God for performing this miracle. But they would have to wait almost fifteen years before they would understand its real impact.

In the meantime Orv wrote his friends the following:

... Elias is strong and healthy and the Secoyas now shake my hand when they greet me. Furthermore, the children of the village scramble around our house as if nothing ever happened. I had hoped the Secoyas would realize their ungrounded fear about touching a dead jaguar when there has been a new birth in the village. My grounds for thinking they would was Elias himself. Everyone can see how strong and healthy he is. But this is not to be.

The Secoyas still cling to this belief, explaining that the reason the child didn't die is because I'm not a Secoya. They firmly believe that had a Secoya touched the dead jaguar, the child would have surely died.

Oh yes, one more thing. Not to be outdone, Mary had her own mini-crisis with the Secoya culture. One day when a group of Secoya women were visiting in our house, Mary jokingly took a stick and began walking like an old woman. She and I thought it was funny; the Secoyas didn't. Later we discovered Mary had unwittingly offended them. To walk with a stick in the manner of an old woman is something they only do at a burial ceremony.

Mary and Orv would find many more astonishing differences between the Secoya culture and their own. Yet they also discovered many similarities—like marriage, family life, and a deep concern about life and death.

It was the Secoyas' preoccupation with death that most immediately affected Orv and Mary, and for good reason. "We know of only three Secoyas over fifty," wrote Orv, "and they are most feeble."

Ecuador's *Oriente* is a place where many die too soon, too suddenly; but few die unexpectedly. If a child survives the rigors of birth and the critical weaning period, he or she faces a lifelong battle against intestinal parasites and epidemics of flu and measles that can wipe out half a village overnight. Some of the Secoyas believe that if one of their people reaches fifty, it is only by special permission of the spirits.

Many factors prevented most Secoyas from living past their late thirties—factors like bodies weakened from excessive drinking and the always-present Anopheles mosquito; almost every Secoya suffered from chronic malaria. Orv was not to be left out.

"Pastaza, Pastaza, this is Cuyabeno calling. Do you read me, do you read me? Come in, please. Over." Willis Kramer, a soft-spoken, sensitive man and an efficient radio operator, was on duty at SIL's radio shack at the army base in Shell Mera. (MAF was also located there and used "Shell Mera" as their call word. To avoid confusion, SIL personnel in the *Oriente* used "Pastaza" as their code word, after the army base and the river that curved through the jungle a quarter of a mile from the small Ecuadorian outpost. A short time later, SIL moved their radio network to their center at Limon Cocha.)

"Orville is running a high temperature and has bad chills. It looks like a severe case of malaria. Can Bob come and fly Orv out to the doctor in Shell?"

"How's your weather?" asked Willis.

"Not too good, but I think it's breaking. Bob should be able to get through."

"I'll relay this message to Bob immediately. Stand by for another radio transmission in thirty minutes. Over and out."

A young, first-term JAARS pilot, Bob Griffin's natural effervescence and good nature gave way to a serious and careful preparation of his aircraft. The plane, christened "City of Chicago," was a Helio Courier specially equipped for flying in extreme weather conditions and in short takeoff and landing situations. Bob had a feeling that this aircraft soon would be called upon to perform to its limit.

Trained to a razor's edge, as are all JAARS pilots, Bob climbed into the cockpit. He strapped himself in, checked the instrument panel, turned the ignition, let the engine warm up, and opened the throttle. As the blue-and-white Helio rushed down the runway, Bob silently asked God to guide him and to break up the heavy clouds.

There are few navigational aids in the Ecuadorian jungle. When a pilot lifts off from a tiny jungle airstrip there, he looks out over a vast sea of giant broccoli-top trees. Only the rivers that ribbon through the thick forests break the monotony of trees. For this reason, JAARS pilots normally flew only visual flight rules—"If you can't see, you don't go." Instrument flight was considered unwise and was forbidden except under extreme emergency conditions.*

Orv's situation constituted an emergency, but not so extreme so as to endanger pilot and plane. There had to be a break in the weather.

Bob took off and began circling the Shell Mera airstrip. In the ominous curtain of gray clouds, Bob spotted a few light spots. Then, suddenly, the ceiling lifted. Visibility was a good five miles, and Bob headed for Cuyabeno.

Cuyabeno is about two hundred miles from Shell Mera. The three-quarter mark on the journey is an island in the middle of the Aguarico River. Bob would first fly up the Napo River, cross over the jungle to the Aguarico, and continue until he saw the island. Spotting this navigational landmark was a must if Bob was to successfully plot his course to the waiting and anxious Mary. But twenty minutes into the hour and a half

*Improved navigational aids currently make limited instrument flight routine.

flight, Bob suddenly hit a solid wall of black cumulous clouds. It would be impossible to spot the small island under these conditions.

It was one thing to have checked the weather at the takeoff and landing sites, but there was no way Bob could know what it was like between the two.

"Pastaza, Pastaza, this is zero four delta; this is zero four delta. Do you read me?"

"Zero four delta, this is Pastaza; zero four delta, this is Pastaza. I read you, come in."

"Pastaza, I've encountered a solid wall of clouds, visibility less than one mile, severe rain, and almost zero ceiling. As soon as I spot a hole I'm going to try to get through underneath."

"Roger, zero four delta," replied Willis. "Report your position every five minutes."

"Going underneath" meant Bob would try to find a break in the thick clouds and spiral the Helio down to fly over the river at treetop level. And that's exactly what he did.

For the next twenty minutes, Bob skillfully guided his plane against a torrential rain that blasted against his plexiglass windshield like trillions of steel pellets. For most of that twenty minutes, the only way he could keep on course was to look straight down and out at the trees that lined the riverbank. (This would be like a person's driving his car in thick fog, guiding himself by hanging his head out the side window and watching the center line.) If it hadn't been for the seriousness of Orv's illness, Bob most certainly would have turned back.

Then, just when he was beginning to wonder if the sun ever shone in the jungle, the plane broke out of the rain clouds and into brilliant sunshine. Immediately

Bob pulled back on the flight controls and nosed the plane up above the broken cumulous clouds.

The break came at just the right time for Bob to cross over from the Napoc River to the Aguarico and spot the small island checkpoint.

"Pastaza, Pastaza. This is zero four delta, this is zero four delta. Do you read me?"

"Zero four delta, zero four delta. This is Pastaza. I read you, come in."

"Pastaza, I've just spotted the island and set a course of 26 degrees. I should reach Cuyabeno in 12 minutes."

Exactly twelve minutes after checking in with Willis, Bob dipped his wings to a waving Mary, circled the tiny clearing, touched down on the short airstrip, and taxied almost to the Johnsons' screened door.

Although the timing was perfect, the weather was not. As Orv walked weakly to the plane and stretched out on an air mattress behind the pilot's seat, black clouds began their menacing approach. Reassuring Mary that Orv would soon be in good hands at the hospital in Shell Mera, Bob again taxied down the airstrip in readiness for takeoff. But every bump and jolt set off violent waves of cracking pain inside Orv's head.

"Pray that the weather holds till we get back to Shell," called Bob to Mary.

"I will, I will," Mary promised. "God go with you!" Mary waved as Bob took off with her young husband, who was cupping his head in his hands.

Mary and other translators and SIL workers prayed, and for almost an hour God held back the weather. But then, Bob flew unavoidably into yet another curtain of gray clouds that stretched as far as the eye could see.

At one point, the turbulence buffeted the tiny plane

with such force that Orv bounced right off the air mattress. The mattress somehow was punctured as the Helio convulsed under the storm's pressure.

This time, however, Bob didn't fly under the clouds. Rather, he chose to sit out the storm on an airstrip at the edge of Auca territory. Auca spears notwithstanding, Bob felt it was safer on the ground than in the air.

For an hour Bob scanned the sky for signs of a break that would allow him to continue his mission of mercy. For Bob, it was an hour of watching and praying that the clouds would rain themselves out. For Orv, it was an hour of incredible misery; he shivered and shook with the malaria that was taking over his body.

Sensing a growing urgency to get Orv under hospital care, Bob once again decided to take off for Shell Mera. Although the rain still struck the plane's windshield, it seemed only a mist compared to what they had been through earlier. Twenty minutes after taking off from the Auca airstrip, Bob made his final approach and touched down at Shell Mera. Almost before the prop had stopped spinning, Orv was whisked away by a waiting doctor.

About this experience, Bob Griffin later wrote:

> After taxiing to the hanger, I slipped out of the cockpit and suddenly realized how exhausted and wrung out I was. I also realized I felt a deep sense of peace, satisfaction, and gratitude to God for getting us through safely. The peace and satisfaction came from being part of the team that serves our translators. The translators are, after all, on the firing line as they struggle to get God's Word to those who still don't have it in their language.

It is interesting that Bob used "firing line" to describe Orv's and Mary's situation. At times during those first five years (and later), the "noise" from the "firing line" became almost unbearable for Mary.

For starters, when baby Omar was fourteen months old, he was joined by a brother—Roger Nathaniel. Orv and Mary named their second son after two of the men who died in an attempt to reach the Aucas. (Roger Youderian had also been Orv's roommate at SIL.) Then, twenty-eight months later, both brothers were introduced to Virginia Ellen, their first and only sister. Their third and final brother, David, was born a year and a half later, in 1959.

As with any mother of four preschool children, Mary was constantly tired. She could only describe those years as "turbulent." In addition to caring for her children's physical needs—feeding them, washing their diapers (without a corner laundromat), and cooking, Mary had the responsibility of a demanding and growing medical work. At one point, two thirds of the village came down with flu, and Orv and Mary were on call twenty-four hours a day. Mary took charge during the day and Orv took the night shift.

In the midst of this almost nonstop activity, Mary felt a loneliness that came not just because she was without the company of her peers (she and Orv once spent eleven months in Cuyabeno without a break), but which sprang from the feelings of inadequacy she still had at times. She wished she was better trained and more prepared for the work she was called to do. Always in the back of her mind was a nagging fear: "What if I am called on to treat a case I can't handle?" (Much later in her life, Mary would overcome her feelings of low self-esteem in a new understanding of an old truth—namely, that God through His Son had *chosen* and *accepted* her just as she was.)

In place of face-to-face contact with friends and colleagues, Mary and Orv wrote letters. After those nonstop eleven months in Cuyabeno, Mary wrote:

> The Secoyas are a most friendly and outgoing people. They're not the least afraid to find out who you are and how you live. When we built our first house, we mistakenly built it without a porch. This meant we always had a roomful of Secoyas, lifting up every lid, tasting everything I cooked, fingering every dress, blouse, blanket, and household item. Even our garbage was examined. I didn't like that.
>
> Then when I came out of the village after eleven straight months I found I could hardly stand city noises. Little things like a slamming door startled me.

To enlarge the scope and vision of their supporting friends, Orv also wrote about village life from his point of view. He told of building a second house to replace the first, which had been built with inferior materials. The new house had screened windows, a metal roof, and of course, a porch. He also told about building the furniture, chairs, table, and even the beds that went into their little frame house. "It makes living so much easier," he wrote.

Orv explained about the ninety-degree heat and the ninety percent humidity that drained their energy like water running through a sieve. In order to survive, they needed ten to eleven hours of rest. But they seldom got it, because a constant stream of people came to their house at all hours with medical problems and other needs.

But Orv struggled with a far greater problem—the Secoya language. For five discouraging years he was unable to analyze the grammatical structure. Both he and

Mary could carry on a conversation in Secoya on a variety of levels, but they couldn't find the pattern of the language.

Then one day Orv began to realize why he had such a problem. There were three dialects in the area and he hadn't separated them. Unknowingly, Orv was in effect working with three structures—all at once! While this understanding helped Orv to better clarify his attack on the language problems, it didn't make the job easier. He still needed to hack his way through a formidable linguistic jungle.

Coupled with this, Orv and Mary faced harrowing sieges of sickness. Although Mary didn't succumb to specific tropical diseases, after David's birth she suffered complications that required hospitalization and extended rest and care. In addition to this and her frequent state of near exhaustion, Mary had to take special care of Roger. The high humidity played havoc with her second son who, as a fifth grader, kept Mary praying through the night watches, wondering if he would survive his repeated asthmatic attacks which were complicated by frequent bouts of nephritis.

As difficult as this was for Mary and Orv to understand, they accepted what God had given them to bear. They often felt like quitting, but never both at the same time. And from out of this crucible of pain, discouragement, and sickness came two people whose mettle was tested. And when they passed the test, their reward was a community of Secoyas who for the first time in their history experienced a living union with the true God of creation, through His Son, Jesus Christ.

Part of this test came embodied in a man wearing a full brown beard and a black cassock.

CHAPTER NINE

More Things That Unite Than Separate

"Everything at Cuyabeno is just about like it was when y'all left for furlough a year ago," drawled the JAARS pilot.

"You mean our house is all in one piece?" said Mary in mock surprise. "It's okay if it isn't," she added. "We don't have much to lose."

"Aren't there any changes out there we should know about?" asked Orv.

"Well, not exactly changes," said the pilot. "But you do have a new resident."

"That's great," said Mary. "Who is he, or is he a she?"

"He's a he, and he comes from Spain. His name is Father Anastacio. He's young, about twenty-eight, quite outgoing. I think you'll get along great. I might add, though, he's rather traditional."

"That doesn't matter," said Orv with a gentle laugh.

"He'll get over that the first time Mary feeds him a batch of her turtle egg pancakes. That's how she got me, you know."

"I know people in Arkansas eat funny things," said the pilot, "but turtle egg pancakes?"

"Oh, come on, you two," grinned Mary. "Don't you think it's about time we quit talking and started flying?"

"We're on our way," said the pilot. "Let's get strapped in."

"Where did you say the father built his house?" asked Mary.

"Right on the end of the airstrip."

"Well, he'll sure know when we're coming and going," Orv said.

"That's not all bad," replied the pilot. "Maybe he'll have a glass of lemonade waiting for us, like Mary always has."

As the pilot had suggested, the priest was there waiting as the Helio Courier touched down on the grassy airstrip. With him were a group of Secoyas. No matter where they were or what they were doing, they always came to greet the arriving or departing plane.

Among the waiting Secoyas was Matilde, her husband Cecilio, her sons Celestino and Elias, and her daughter Celinda. Since that day when Mary smacked Elias on the back and saved him from choking, this family had become close friends with Mary and Orv. Matilde was especially close to Mary, and while she was on furlough she frequently prayed for God to reveal Himself to Matilde and her family.

Now here they were, all smiles and hugs and caught up in the excited chatter of trying to catch up on a year's news all at once. The welcoming scene was a happy one.

124

Then Mary noticed that Father Anastacio was standing apart from the rest, unsmiling.

Thus began the most curious three years in all of the Johnsons' ministry among the Secoyas in Cuyabeno. In time, whenever the father returned from a trip to another village Mary would welcome him with a tall glass of lemonade. He was usually reluctant to receive her hospitality, but the heat and humidity tipped the scales in her favor. In many ways, it was an important growing and stretching experience for the priest and for Mary.

At first, Mary found Father Anastacio an intrusion into "their" work. She learned through the grapevine that he had forbidden a number of Secoyas to visit the Johnsons. One of these was a fourteen-year-old girl who had worked for Mary, and of whom Mary was particularly fond. Mary was upset to discover that he could in a few short weeks disturb the rapport and confidence that had taken her and Orv five years to build. She was also angry when she noticed that at every opportunity the priest avoided walking past their house, even if it meant he had to go out of his way to do so.

But because she is who she is, she couldn't keep the fires of anger and resentment burning for long. Before too many weeks had passed, the Lord impressed on Mary that Father Anastacio was in reality a lonely young man. After all, he had no family; he lived alone in a strange environment and he was unfamiliar with Secoya language and culture.

"Looks like you're making a birthday cake," said seven-year-old Omar one afternoon.

"It is," said Mary.

"Oh goody. Is it Daddy's?"

"No, it's for Father Anastacio and I want you and Roger to go down and ask him to come for supper at five o'clock."

"How did you know it was his birthday today?" asked Omar.

"I have ways of finding these things out," replied Mary mysteriously. "Now go invite him for supper."

The children returned in a short while. "He says he won't come."

"Did you tell him I made a special cake for his birthday?"

"Yep, we did, and he still said he wouldn't come."

"Well, that's all right, you just go once more and tell him the table is all set with a place for him. Tell the father we are all waiting for him to come and eat his cake."

This time they returned with the father in tow. The meal was outstanding—roast wild meat, rice, yams, and delicious turtle soup made from turtles from the nearby river. And of course, there was cake. The table conversation was mostly small talk—where Mary and Orv had grown up, how they met, and why they had come to Ecuador.

When the meal was finished, Orv passed Father Anastacio their Catholic Bible and asked him to read a passage.

"You mean you read the Bible?" asked the priest.

"Yes, we do," Orv said. "It's one of the most important elements in our lives."

"If we can talk about it more," said Mary, "you would understand there are more things that unite us than separate us. We have nothing in common with the

126

village shaman. But there are many things we have in common with you."

"Do you believe in the Virgin Mary?" asked the father.

"Of course we believe Mary was a virgin," answered Mary.

"Well then, let's talk," he replied.

It was dark when Father Anastacio left the Johnson home. Carefully, with the aid of an old flashlight, he picked his way over the trail and through the village toward his hut. He had sensed that the Johnsons were genuinely interested in him as a person; it had been a long time since anyone wanted to know about his personal life. It had been good to remember his childhood and his years as a seminarian. And when he had talked of his mother, the warmth inside had mingled with the bittersweet pain of missing her.

Inside his hut, he stretched out on his canvas cot, a leftover from an army surplus store. Lying there in the darkness and listening to the baritone croaking of tree frogs, he sighed. When he had said goodnight, he had told Orv and Mary that he was impressed with their faith. He had even said he wished he could be like them.

He himself had quietly come to the conclusion that the Secoyas were incapable of understanding the metaphysical aspects of Jesus Christ and God. In a word, he believed the Secoyas could never become Christians.

He didn't share this conviction with Orv or Mary, but he was impressed that they believed God's salvation was capable of reaching any and all peoples if they once had the opportunity to read or hear the gospel story in their native language. He admitted to himself it was an interesting idea. "I wish I could believe like you, Mary," he had said. "But I can't. And I can't be friends with you. People in the village will think we are the same." And Mary had smiled.

It may have been Father Anastacio's intention to remain aloof, but in reality he did become a friend to the whole family. Frequently, when Mary would ask Omar and Roger where they were going they would answer offhandedly, "Oh, we think we'll go visit our priest."

There were, of course, more suppers and cakes and turtle egg pancakes. And occasionally when Mary ran out of supplies, especially powdered milk for the children, Father Anastacio graciously supplied their needs from his supplies.

Then there were the conversations. Some were serious, examining in detail the differences and similarities of their respective faiths. There was also conversation that relaxed and soothed nerves after a long day of treating people's cuts and sores, or after teaching a reading class, or after an exacting translation session.

Thus the weeks and months and years passed. Each went about his work, believing himself to be a participant in the Creator's purposes.

"Señora! Señora! Please come with your medicines. It's my daughter Aurora. She is in great pain!"

"Pain? What kind of pain?" asked Mary.

The woman's voice was a mixture of agony, anger, fear, and near hysteria as she said, "The pain is the pain of demons! They have come to take my Aurora away."

"No, no," assured Mary, trying to comfort and calm the woman. "Your daughter will not die. Jesus is stronger and has more power than any demons. Let's go quickly to your house."

The discovery Mary and Orv made when they first entered the woman's house was most disquieting. Secretly, Orv, and to some extent Mary, had believed the mother's diagnosis of her daughter's problem was exaggerated. But any doubts Mary might have had evaporated immediately when she began to treat Aurora.

Once a carefree young woman, Aurora now lay curled up on a raised plank bed, frightened as a week-old fawn. In a half-whimpering cry and with her once dark, lustrous eyes glazed and staring into some unseen world, Aurora kept repeating, "The devil is going to take me, the devil is going to take me, the devil is going to take me . . ."

Quietly Mary sat on the bed and prayed silently. Then she said, "No, no, precious Aurora, the devil is not going to take you. You are just a little sick, and I am going to give you some medicine, and soon you'll be well. Nothing, nothing is going to harm you."

Mary gave Aurora one last gentle touch of reassurance, got up from the bed, and turned to speak with the mother. But before Mary finished her first sentence, Aurora uttered a violent scream and fell convulsing to the *chonta* palm floor. Mary rushed to her, but not before Aurora had inflicted vicious scratches on her cheeks, neck, and shoulders. Mary managed to give her a sedative, but half an hour later Aurora was still screaming and convulsing on the floor.

"There is no doubt," Mary said to Orv. "Aurora is possessed by demons. There is nothing medically that I can do to help her."

Realizing the severity of the problem, Mary and Orv radioed the Limon Cocha center and asked for special prayer that God would break the power of fear and superstition that Satan had inflicted on the Secoyas. Most of all, they asked prayer for Aurora, that she be restored to her right mind and that the demons be expelled from her mind and body. Mary then returned to offer what help she could to Aurora and her parents.

"You're right," said Mary to Aurora's mother when she returned. "Your daughter is possessed by an evil spirit. The only way she can be released from this power is to pray and ask Jesus to help us."

"What good will that do?" asked Aurora's father. "Jesus is not God. The moon is god. The only way my daughter will be healed and brought back is to drink the *yahe*. This drink will help us see visions. And when we see the visions given to us by the *yahe*, we will know how to appease the demons. And the one who can tell us best how to appease the demons is Fernando. Fernando is both the greatest shaman and the greatest chief of all the Secoyas. I will summon him to drink the *yahe* in the religious house at the edge of our village."

And so Fernando was called, and indeed he did appease the demon and Aurora was released. It was at this point that Orv and Mary understood in a new way the truth of Ephesians 6:12:

> For we do not wrestle against flesh and blood, but against principalities, against powers, against the rulers of the darkness of this age, against spiritual wickedness in the heavenly places.

And from this experience Orv and Mary had a new resolve to earnestly ask God to answer their prayers.

Seven years later, Mary was to encounter Fernando's hold on the people in a similar situation. This time it was Matilde and Cecilio's daughter, Celinda, who was stricken with demons. And as before, Fernando was called.

Mary had met Fernando. He was a small, unimpressive man, yet she knew he was feared above all other local shamans. Whenever she had an occasion to ask about Fernando, the Secoyas without exception would tell her that he alone was more powerful than any other Shaman. For this reason none dared to cross him.

"I know Fernando is great among you," said Mary, "but I must tell you that the greatest above Fernando and above the moon and all demons and evil spirits— and Satan himself—is Jesus Christ. He alone is God's Son, and He alone has the power to overcome Satan.

"Fernando works his power from himself and for selfish gain, to hold people in fear. But Jesus is stronger because He comes to us in love. And you and all the Secoyas can have this power and freedom from fear just by asking Jesus to enter into your mind and heart. It is Jesus alone who has conquered death, and He alone can deliver us from fear."

Even when Mary saw how easily Cecilio dismissed her words and returned to his chanting to the moon and his blowing over his daughter in an effort to blow away the evil spirit, she refused to believe the Secoyas would forever be bound by hopelessness. By faith, she and Orv had come to Ecuador and to the Secoya people for this very purpose. They did not want to destroy what was good or meaningful in Secoya culture. Rather, they had come to give the Secoyas an alternative to their spiritual exploitation; to open a new door of freedom, joy, and liberation from Satan's subhuman bondage. Life could be more for the Secoyas than just accident and fate.

Mary knew and believed this with all her heart. Yet running through her mind, put there by the very enemy she was praying God would defeat, was the old self-doubt and feelings of inadequacy. Her one encouragement was that Cecilio had, at least temporarily, refrained from calling on Fernando for help.

"Perhaps," reasoned Mary, "when they see God's power displayed, they will become believers."

About midnight, after an exhausting day of prayer and witnessing, Mary, Matilde, and Cecilio received their first hint that Celinda was being released from the demons. Suddenly Celinda sat up and said in a clear, coherent voice, "I'm going to be all right." But almost immediately she screamed, "Oh, they're coming for me again!"

Then her eyes glazed over. Heavy beads of perspiration appeared on her forehead, and she lapsed into a coma and stopped breathing. Mary rushed to her side and began mouth-to-mouth resuscitation. For two anxious, heart-stopping minutes, Mary breathed her own breath into Celinda's lungs. Then, just as suddenly as she had stopped breathing, Celinda began to breathe normally, although she was still comatose.

"You see, Jesus is not God as you say He is," accused Cecilio. "This time I am going to blow the clay horn and summon Fernando. He alone can bring my daughter back."

Meanwhile, Matilde had lost all hope that Mary or Jesus or even Fernando could help Celinda. In a pitiful voice filled with despair and anger, she began a long, painful death wail for her daughter.

Mary knew it would be at least two hours before Fernando, who lived some distance away, would arrive by canoe in Cuyabeno. The conch-like sound of the clay horn was used when people were lost in the jungle, or for summoning the shamans. Remarkably, Secoyas living two to three hours away by canoe are able to hear the sound of the horn and interpret the sender's meaning.

Fernando would come soon to drink the *yahe* and work his witchcraft over Celinda. And just as the magicians and sorcerers in Moses' time duplicated some of his miracles,* Mary knew there was a possibility that Fernando's witchcraft could release Celinda from the demons. Although Mary wanted the best for Celinda, she did not want the Secoyas to be continually duped by satanic bondage.

With a faith that refused to be dimmed by the facts, Mary prayed one last prayer: "Lord, before Fernando gets here to work his witchcraft, please give deliverance to Celinda. I pray this so all Secoyas will know it was You and not Fernando who healed Celinda. I pray this also so all Secoyas will know that Your power is greater than Satan and all the demons that ever were."

For the next several hours Mary sat by Celinda's side, praying that God would delay Fernando's coming and that He would work a miracle in Celinda's life. Then, just at dawn, Mary heard excited chatter in the distance, and she knew Fernando had arrived. The sounds of the welcoming party grew louder and louder, until Fernando was at the foot of the notched pole ladder that led up to where Mary sat with Celinda.

Just as Fernando was about to climb the ladder, Celinda woke up. Her eyes were clear, her hands and forehead were cool, and her voice was clear and strong.

From the steadiness of Celinda's voice, Mary could tell

---

*Exodus 7:8–12.

that God had indeed answered prayers and she stood up and spoke to Celinda's father.

"Here is your daughter, well. The demons have left and she is going to be all right. Everything is fine. But I want you to know it was Jesus who delivered her. Fernando the shaman is coming, but I want you to know that your daughter is already delivered." Mary gave Celinda one final hug and then left, passing Fernando on the way out.

Mary and Orv were unaware of the impact Celinda's restoration was making on the Secoyas. All day long, her parents received visitors who looked at their daughter in amazement. She had been delivered without the use of Fernando's witchcraft! But more than that, Celinda was sitting up, talking, and best of all—eating! Everyone recognized the particular kind of demon that had taken possession of Celinda, and they knew that those who had been delivered in the past never ate anything until four days had passed.

Early that same afternoon, Father Anastacio packed his few belongings and set off down river in a dugout canoe. He had received word his mother was dying of cancer and was returning to Spain. Mary and Orv stood on the riverbank and waved their farewells. Time, dialogue, and shared concerns had fused a friendship that was now to be broken forever.

A few weeks later, Mary's faith in God's power was wonderfully strengthened. An experience with an older woman, María, showed her that Satan's stronghold was not impregnable. When Mary was asked to fill in for a short time at the Limon Cocha clinic, she invited María to go with her and Orv to the center and continue as their language teacher. María agreed. After all, how many Secoya women her age had the opportunity to ride in the "sky canoe"?

At Limon Cocha, María and the Johnsons quickly worked into a routine. While Mary worked mornings at the clinic, Orv studied and worked on language materials. The routine worked well until one day when Mary came home and found María in deep distress.

"I'm so sick," she said. "Every time I work on Scripture verses I feel the demons eating me. I'm dying. Get a shaman to do something for me."

"Do you remember Celinda?" asked Mary.

"Yes, yes. I remember how the demons attacked her. Her mother told me how she passed out with the pain of the attacking demon. And this will happen to me if we don't get to a shaman."

"María, María," said Mary gently. "When Celinda had the demon, I told her about the One who is greater than all evil power and greater than all the demons. His name is Jesus Christ, God's Son. If you ask Jesus to come into your heart and be your friend, He will destroy the power of this demon. But Jesus can only come into your heart if you want Him to. Would you, María, like Jesus to be your friend and care for you and defeat the power of this demon?"

"Yes, I would like that," said María. "Then He can deliver me from this demon."

It was a simple request, made with almost microscopic faith, yet it was faith nonetheless. And God has promised to freely forgive anyone who chooses to obey and follow Him. In that instant, María experienced God's free gift of saving grace and eternal life through Jesus Christ.

Mary and Orv knew there was a great deal María

would have to learn. They also knew she would have to bear the burden of being one of the first active Secoya believers in Cuyabeno. The burden would be doubly difficult as she was Fernando's mother-in-law! But María learned with greater insight than Mary expected. On one occasion several weeks after this incident, Mary carefully explained the Crucifixion story. When she finished, old María was silent for a moment, then said thoughtfully, "What a price to pay for our salvation!"

Thus María became the first Secoya among a nation of more than six hundred to render obedience to her Creator and to experience the great truth that she was no longer under the burden and bondage of sin, fear, and the torment of emptiness.

In this seventh year among the Secoyas, the first Secoya man also understood this gospel Mary and Orv were talking about. His name was Celestino. When he entered into a personal, obedient relationship with Jesus Christ, people in Cuyabeno laughed—especially Fernando. He ridiculed Celestino, taunting him for accepting the white man's religion.

For four more years, Celestino stood alone as a believer among the men of his village. And for those years, Fernando continued to laugh and sneer at his nephew for walking in this new way of life.

But then Fernando's mother-in-law, María, died. Her funeral was unlike any Secoya funeral before. One could sense a strange restfulness, a peace and confidence, an absence of fear, nor did she want her belongings placed beside her in the grave. At this, Fernando was both puzzled and intrigued.

CHAPTER TEN

Just Being Themselves

Before the time when Fernando decided he too wanted to walk the new way his nephew Celestino was walking, many changes took place in Cuyabeno. Perhaps the greatest change came in 1972, when the village moved to what is now the village of San Pablo.

The jungle around Cuyabeno was under water about half the year, and the soil was drained of its nutrients. In San Pablo, the Secoyas had better land to farm and they did not have to rely on turtle eggs as an important part of their diet.

Due to Mary's nursing skills, fewer people now died, and the population of Cuyabeno had grown from about 50 to more than 120. There were just too many people for the surrounding jungle to support in its natural state, and as game and turtle eggs became scarce the

Secoyas began traveling farther and farther away from their homes to find food.

Not only would heads of families go on long foraging trips, but entire families would leave for weeks and sometimes months. The men and boys of the village were always trying to find work. They needed money for knives, fishhooks and line, and ammunition for their guns. And when the jungle became hunted out, they could no longer get hides to sell.

Over the years, Orv quietly explained to the Secoyas how they could build up the soil with humus. He also introduced some chickens and a few goats. Since the Secoyas moved frequently, it was difficult for them to care properly for the chickens, and many were lost to predators.

But when the Secoyas moved to San Pablo, things progressed quickly, both socioeconomically and spiritually. After Orv and Mary built a small home, Orv set about clearing the jungle to prepare the land for farming and pasture. He gave the Secoyas simple instruction in better farming methods and helped them to secure domestic animals. There were only a few at first—five heifers, six goats, and a Duroc boar to upgrade the hogs. Orv wanted the goats to help keep back the jungle and undesirable brush from the pastures.

Change is a fact of life even in remote jungle areas, and Orv wanted to prepare the Secoyas to meet the inevitable confrontation with the outside world. He acted upon an ethic he considered an integral part of his personal faith, namely, reaching out in tangible ways to the whole man. What better way, he reasoned, than to introduce new economic options in the form of community development.

This desire for a holistic approach to the gospel sprang from his Arkansas roots. The memory of his Spanish-American War veteran father plowing the rock-infested, stump-filled homestead with a flop-eared mule was forever stamped on Orv's subconscious mind. But more than that, Orv never forgot the pain of having to sell their farm to a government land and development program. There was almost no land to farm and his father died early, so the family had existed on Orv's and his brother's skill in hunting rabbits.

Coupled with the Johnsons' concern for the Secoyas' physical and economic well-being was their concern for the people's spiritual well-being. As the community development program grew, so did the number of believers.

One of the most significant Christian families among the Secoyas is Matilde and her husband Cecilio. Their son, Celestino, the first Secoya man to accept the gospel, is now the school teacher and a leader in the San Pablo church. Their other son, Elias, who was a baby when the Johnsons first went to the Secoyas, the one whose life Mary once saved when he was choking to death, is a fine, well-grounded Christian and co-translator. Elias still carries the deep burden of completing the translation. Elias's wife runs the local dispensary in San Pablo.

And what of Fernando, Matilde's brother? After much prayer and patient sharing of their faith, Matilde and Cecilio won him to the Lord. They will tell you that he was a formidable shaman, but not too formidable for God to reach.

Matilde's Christian influence in the village of San Pablo reaches out in many other ways. Like several other Secoyas, she came to faith in Christ by the witness and ministry of her son Celestino, while Orv and Mary were on furlough.

Until she became a believer, Matilde had been deeply afraid of becoming sick and of dying. One day after she had given her fears to God, Matilde sent a tape to Mary. In a soft, weak voice quite unlike her normal effervescent self, she told Mary she had a bleeding ulcer and was going into the hospital in Quito for an operation.

"I want you to know," said Matilde, "that I go into the hospital believing everything is in the hands of our Lord. He has the power to raise me, or He can take me."

Matilde was admitted and examined by an intern. He said to her, "Woman, take a long look at the mountains."

"Why do you tell me this?" asked Matilde.

"Because your ulcer is so bad I don't think you'll survive the surgery. Abdominal surgery is a major operation, and you are not strong enough to go through such a traumatic experience and survive."

Matilde laughed. "Doctor," she said, "you don't know my God. I have already talked to Him, and I *know* I will survive."

The surgery was extensive; they removed most of her stomach. But as Matilde had predicted, she survived. Amazed that she had lived through it, the doctors placed her on a strict diet, explaining that it would take many days for her to heal. But within days after the operation, the doctors were again amazed as they noticed Matilde was recovering much faster than they had thought possible.

A woman who had been in the hospital for a month noticed Matilde's rapid progress and asked her for help.

"I see you are getting better faster than I am," she said. "Can you send for your shaman and get me some

140

of that enchanted liquid or whatever it is you are drinking to make you well? I have been here so long, and still I don't even have the strength to walk. I can't seem to get well."

"Just a moment," said Matilde. "I will come and talk to you."

When Matilde walked over to the woman's bedside, she took her hand and said, "I no longer live believing that the shaman's enchanted liquid can make me well. Once I lived that way. I believed the devil and the shaman could make me well. And it is true that sometimes the devil cured us. But now Jesus Christ is the One I pray to. He has more strength than anyone. And He truly loves us. Do you want me to pray for you?"

"Yes," said the woman. "Please pray for me."

Matilde placed her arm around the woman and prayed a beautiful little prayer: "Lord, You made me. You made this woman. You know how to heal. We know You gave us medicine and we thank You for that. But, Lord, we are trusting You to heal this woman because the medicine doesn't seem to work. I know that when You heal this woman, she is going to thank You a lot."

And God did just as Matilde asked. The next day this woman, who hadn't had the strength to get up out of bed for a month, stood and began to walk the halls.

After Matilde's recovery, she began a ministry of loving care for the sick and elderly of San Pablo. By her own admission she was formerly a selfish, ungiving woman, a woman who was angry most of the time—angry with herself, with her husband, and with anyone who happened to come into the village for a visit. Now she says, "Jesus Christ has taken the anger out of mv heart."

Mary considers her a faithful prayer partner Once

during a hard time when Mary lost her brothers Stannie and David in the same car accident, Matilde ministered to and encouraged Mary in a beautiful, caring way by sending her a cassette tape while Mary was in the States.

And then there was Cesario, a big man for a Secoya with an ego and swaggering sense of self-importance to match his size. When Mary first began to talk to Cesario about the Lord, he cut her short. "Don't tell me any more. I know more than you do. Besides, that Bible of yours is too small to be of any importance. If your book were truly a message from God, it would be *much* bigger." And then Cesario would proceed to tell Mary all about the visions he had seen and how important he was because he drank the *yahe*. But slowly—like Matilde, Cecilio, and their sons Elias and Celestino—Cesario also came to faith in Jesus Christ.

Some time after Cesario became grounded in his faith, God used him in a unique way. With his wife, his teen-age son, and another woman, they moved from living near the Peruvian border to be near the group of believers in San Pablo. Late in the afternoon on the third day of this five-day trip, the little band was camped for the night on a small river sandbar when suddenly a plane came in so low that Cesario could see the pilot.

Unknown to Cesario, the six-passenger de Haviland Beaver carried an important Colombian air force colonel—the commander of all of Colombia's southern forces. With the colonel were two other officers and the pilot. Toward the end of the day, the plane had flown into bad weather and premature darkness. Blown off course and unable to find their destination, the pilot unknowingly flew into Ecuadorian territory.

At that point the situation was critical. They were low

on fuel, it was dark, and they had no idea where they were. Then, from out of nowhere, the pilot spotted an unknown river and began to follow it. The colonel and pilot agreed that their chances of survival were better if they landed on the river than in the jungle.

While they discussed their options, the pilot suddenly spotted a large sandbar in the middle of the river. He set the plane down, but the landing was hard, and as the pilot feverishly tried to avoid clumps of brush, rocks and other debris, the wheels of the de Haviland sank into the soft sand and the plane flipped over on its back. No one was hurt, but the colonel and his crew believed they had come down in the middle of savage Indian territory, and they were frightened!

Cesario and his group heard the plane cough and sputter as it passed over their heads.

"Ah," said Cesario sadly, "the plane will have an accident. Let us pray for those inside. Tomorrow we must look for them. If they are dead, we must bury them properly."

Early the next morning, Cesario and his group started out to look for the downed plane. All that day they paddled around one bend after another, through rapids and heavy currents. But when nightfall came, they still hadn't found the wreckage.

Earlier than the day before, they began their second day of searching. Two hours later, Cesario saw the colonel and his crew sitting on the sandbar beside the overturned plane. Cesario smiled, silently thanking God for the survival of those he thought would surely be dead.

When the pilot and the colonel saw this giant of a man in a long *cushma*, his face painted with red achiote dye and a brightly feathered crown on his head, they were

143

terrified! Fearing for their lives, the frightened men watched as Cesario sprang from his canoe, beached it, then strode up to them with his hand extended.

In halting Spanish Cesario said, "We are Evangelicals. We saw your plane two nights ago and have been praying for you. We are so happy that God has spared your lives. Let us give thanks together to God for saving you." There was only the sound of the river at his back and the soft jungle breezes whispering through the trees as Cesario prayed to the God of heaven.

The Secoyas, like most ethnic groups, have been exploited and treated with rudeness and contempt by those who don't speak their language or who don't care to understand them as people. Yet Cesario, who himself had been a self-seeking and sometimes obnoxious troublemaker, said to the men, "Come, I have shot a wild turkey, and my wife will prepare food for you."

The colonel and his men, who had been stunned at the thought of encountering savage Indians, were now equally stunned at what was taking place before their eyes. Cesario added that after they had eaten he would secure the plane with ropes, in case the river rose rapidly. "And I will guard your plane while my son takes you to an outpost that has a radio where you can be picked up by helicopter." Amazingly, as they paddled for seventeen straight hours to the outpost, not once did they see another sandbar!

The colonel promised Cesario's son a reward for what he and his father had done. "We truly owe our lives to you," he said.

The colonel was as good as his word. About a month later Wycliffe's Ecuador Director, Don Johnson (no relation to Orv), received a request from Wycliffe's Colombia Director. Could he get in touch with a Secoya man named Cesario? Don Johnson was surprised to learn that this request had come from a high-ranking Colombian colonel.

Mary and Orv arranged a rendezvous point, and Cesario paddled his canoe there to receive his reward. And what a reward it was! Besides forty bolts of material, the colonel had given Cesario a radio, a gun, flashlights, pots and pans, and a number of machetes.

"Isn't it great that the colonel and his men thanked you in this way?" asked Mary.

"Just think," answered Cesario, "The greater reward is in heaven."

These are just a few stories of how God has worked in the lives of the Secoyas through the twenty-five-year ministry of Orv and Mary—their witness, the Bible translation, Mary's nursing skills, and Orv's community development programs. But perhaps if Celestino—the first Secoya man to believe in Jesus Christ—shares his testimony, we will all have a clearer picture of God at work in His world.

When I was young, I knew nothing of the Word of God. I had not even heard that God's Word existed! I did my own will and chose my own pleasures—like drinking, dancing, and fighting. Oh, I was proud of my strength. Nobody could overcome me. In addition to this, my friends and relatives had many opportunities to go to the shaman and drink *yahe*. When I drank the *yahe*, it made me prouder because I was starting to see visions, and my Uncle Fernando was beginning to teach me how to become a shaman.

Then after a while I became ill. However, when I drank the *yahe* I felt well. I found that when I stopped drinking it I felt ill again, in pain and cut off from everyone. My life was sad, and my only interest was in becoming a shaman and hurting others.

From age twelve to fourteen I drank the *yahe*, as did my mother and father. At that time I was helping Orv Johnson with Bible translation work. Again I went after my own pleasure. There seemed to be nothing else in life but drinking and fighting. In all that I was doing my heart became hardened. Yet I knew I was looking for something to give me reality and peace.

When I was sixteen something happened to my eyes and I couldn't see too well. I asked my Uncle Fernando, the shaman, to cure me. "The only cure I have," he said, "is the *yahe*." But when I drank it, it made me ill. It seemed as though I was out of my mind. I knew I was ill, my parents knew I was ill, and they too tried to cure me. They couldn't and they were sad.

One day in the Johnson house there was a leaflet on the table of the study where I was working. I opened the leaflet and lay back in my hammock. There were some words from John 3:16: "For God so loved the world that He gave his only begotten Son, that whoever believes in Him shall not perish but have eternal life." I thought deeply about these words and read them again.

I thought about the things Orv had said and about the customs of my ancestors and how I tried to follow them. Then I thought, "Why should I follow the customs of the old ones? All I get is weakness and sickness." In that moment I said to myself, "From now on I will not take part in things that will hurt me or things that will hurt others."

Then I began to pray as I have never prayed before. "Lord, I believe that You are listening to my voice here in the sunshine. I believe You are here. Set me free; I don't want to be like I was before. I want to be Your servant. I give You my body and my spirit."

I prayed some more words, and then I wept, and I wept harder than I had ever wept in my youth. I then finished my prayer, saying, "I who was lost in your sight, I give myself to You. I who am very weak, receive me." At that moment I was filled with joy. All day long I remembered my prayer and I was happy. I knew the Lord had received me as one of His children.

There is much more that could be written about Celestino, Cesario, Fernando, Elias, Matilde, Cecilio—and of course, Mary and Orv. Perhaps one day it will be told in another book.

Why has the Lord worked this way among the Secoyas? I do not pretend to know the mind of God. However, the Spirit works through human channels. The growth of the village of San Pablo from twenty-four people to over two hundred, with ninety percent of them active believers in Jesus Christ, is due in part to two things.

First, Mary and Orv allowed the church to develop within Secoyan cultural patterns, never forcing their own values or interpretations of the Scriptures on the people. Second, and equally important, were Mary's and Orv's attitudes and lifestyle before the Secoyas.

Matilde once told Mary why so many Secoyas were convinced that Jesus Christ loves them.

You came to us and lived among us in the same kind of house we lived in. You ate the same kind of food we did. When we worked for you you paid us a fair wage and were always true to your word. And when we were sick you cared for us with a love we could feel. When we were hurt or frightened you touched us and listened to us.

147

You told us that God was love, and that Jesus Christ was more powerful than all the spirits that dwell in Secoyaland. We listened to these words, but it was not so much the words that convinced us that what you said was true about God. Rather, it was how you lived among us that convinced us that what you said about God and His Son Jesus must be true.

"By just being themselves," said Bill Anders and Roy Gleason, observers and longtime friends of the Johnsons, "Mary and Orv preached truth through their personalities. With all their feelings of weakness, discouragements, family problems, and faltering faith, they still have reached out and touched a people. They are living examples of what the work of Wycliffe Bible Translators is all about. And they have given the Secoyas the most precious and meaningful of all gifts—the very words of God in their own Secoya language."

EPILOGUE:

Summing Up

I first met Mary Johnson at a dinner party, the very afternoon I arrived in Quito, Ecuador in September, 1978. My host and hostess for the party were Ecuador Director Don Johnson and his wife Helen. (There is no blood relationship between the two Johnson families, but Don and Helen have a deep love and caring friendship for Orv and Mary that approximates and often goes beyond the caring of a natural family.)

For many years Don, a handsome Swede from the state of Washington, and his equally striking wife, Helen, had invited me to come to Ecuador and "write a story." But there always seemed to be another project that prevented my coming. In February, 1978, I attended a meeting in Lima, Peru, where I heard Don tell about Cesario and the plane incident. That was exciting in itself. But when I began to investigate the background, and learned about my longtime friend and colleague Marianna Slocum's involvement with Mary when she first went to Mexico, I knew there was a story just begging to be written.

Five days after I met Mary at Don and Helen's home on that quiet street in Quito, Ecuador, Mary and I left for Limon Cocha and San Pablo. I had spent every morning and most afternoons and early evenings quizzing Mary, getting facts straight, probing for stories, and prodding Mary to reach back into her past for more specific information.

Now it was time to meet Orv. He had stayed out in San Pablo, and he monitored our flight from Limon Cocha to the San Pablo airstrip on his two-way radio. (Once we reached San Pablo we still had a half hour walk through the jungle to the Johnson home.)

The weather is always a factor when taking off from or landing on jungle airstrips, but on this day it seemed there would be no problems. It was bright and clear both in Limon Cocha and in San Pablo. But when we were five minutes from San Pablo, we flew straight into a severe storm front.

There was no lightning—just heavy pellets of rain and smoky black clouds. We circled the airstrip, a short ribbon of grass cut out of the thick jungle, and saw a tiny cluster of people below. "That will be Matilde down there," said Mary from the back seat.

"Well, she's going to have to wait a little to greet you," said the pilot. "We're going to have to fly a holding pattern until the winds blow the clouds clear of the strip."

For the next few minutes we flew a pattern that took

us out over the jungle through the wispy clouds. And then, wonder of wonders, a hole of bright sunshine opened up before us and we landed. On the ground, Mary ran into another storm—Matilde! It was a storm of joy and hugs and excited conversation.

"Matilde says she and the others prayed and asked the Lord to push away the clouds so we could land," said Mary. *Amazing,* I thought. *God did indeed push away the clouds. Thank You, Father.*

The JAARS pilot taxied his Helio Courier to the end of the runway, turned around, and roared back down the soggy strip, kicking up a heavy spray of water as he took off into a patchwork of blue sky and wispy black clouds. I watched until I could see him no more, then turned just in time to see Mary, Matilde, and the other Secoyas step onto a narrow trail and disappear into thick jungle greenery.

I hurried after them, my camera bag bumping against me in time with my steps. The trail led me into a large, meadow-like clearing, but then it ended abruptly. For a moment I was confused. There was nothing to guide me or suggest the direction I should take.

And then I saw Mary, standing in the middle of the clearing. It had begun to rain again, and someone had provided her with a poncho—the perfect companion to the mid-calf rubber boots she was wearing. The poncho was like a World War II vintage, green rubber with a hood and drawstrings. It was too big for her; the hood was askew, almost covering her pixie face. She sensed my bewilderment and beckoned me to follow her. There were no words, just a warm smile beaming out from under that rumpled poncho and then simultaneously she bowed from her waist and with a long gracious sweep of her delicate arm, indicated the direction we should take. Never in all my life have I had a more gracious invitation into someone's life and experience.

I think also of Marianna and her partner, Florence Gerdel. As a result of their combined ministry of Bible translation for the highland and lowland Tzeltals, over 22,000 have become believers in Jesus Christ. These are the very people who Stanford Morison once warned Bill Bentley were too savage and unpredictable to try to reach with the Good News.

Across a luncheon table in Dallas, Texas, I interviewed Marianna while she waited for a visa to return to Colombia and her work among the Paéz people. I asked her what God was currently teaching her. "You never get beyond the point of learning to trust the Lord more," she answered. "Right now I am trusting Him to work out the problem of getting back into Colombia, and for help in the printing of the Paéz New Testament." (Marianna had just that morning turned over her third New Testament to the printing arts department at Wycliffe's Dallas headquarters.)

I think of Marianna's parents, Mr. and Mrs. Slocum (now deceased). Even when they were separated from their daughter by many miles they were nevertheless actively involved in an effective prayer ministry for Marianna, Florence, and the Tzeltal people.

As of this writing, Elodia is a bright eighty-seven-year-old. She lives in a modest house in a San Diego suburb with her son-in-law and daughter Margarita. Like Mary, Margarita also lived with the Slocums and received the benefit of a Christian home and an American education. She is currently an office administrator.

When I asked Elodia the same question I asked

Marianna, she smiled and said, "I'm learning from the Scriptures how important it is to be patient. I also am learning that when someone offends me, I am to forgive them, and I am learning more and more I must pray for and try to help those who have offended me."

It had been Elodia's dream to return to New York, and at age eighty-five, she did just that.

"I am amazed," she says, "that a little person like me from a simple town in southern Mexico has been allowed to know Jesus Christ and to live such a rich life, and that my children also know and serve the Lord. God's grace and mercy to me is overwhelming."

Mary echoes her mother's feelings about being overwhelmed with God's grace and love to her. She is grateful that her children are engaged in meaningful work. Omar, their eldest son, is currently doing post graduate work in philosophy at the University of Minnesota. Roger, son number two, is also at the University of Minnesota and will soon graduate in electronic engineering. Ginger is married to Roy Hammond, and they have a desire to serve the Lord however He leads. David, son number three, anticipates a career in missionary maintenance and is presently in a two-and-a-half year training program in Coshocton, Ohio.

Mary is eternally grateful to God for Orv. "God knew the very man I needed," she says. "Orv is strong, quiet, practical, and never looks back. God knew I needed that kind of partner to help me."

I asked Celestino the same question I had asked Marianna and Elodia. When Mary interpreted my question, his eyes brightened. Even his high cheek bones seemed to smile, and he answered with vibrancy and enthusiasm.

"I am here before you," he replied, "only because of

God's love, brought to me through the Johnsons and through God's Word. And now I tell my people, among many other things, that Jesus Christ came to us because of our need for Him. And if we can't sleep at night because of demon activity, we have only to call on Him. He will give us sleep and make our hearts glad.

"I am learning, too, that the Lord does not want any of us to despise those who do not believe as we do about God and Jesus. We are to love such people and think kindly of them.

"Also I am learning about the liberty that comes from God alone. I could seek wealth; I could be a proud man because I am a school teacher and I know more than others in the village. But I know this would not please God my Father or the Lord Jesus Christ. It is my desire that we all here in San Pablo be a company of people who together will hear God speak to us, and after hearing Him speak, will be not only hearers of His Word and voice, but doers also.

"It is my desire that all of us here obey the words of 1 Peter 3:8,9: 'You should be like one big happy family, full of sympathy toward each other, loving one another with tender hearts and humble minds. Don't repay evil for evil. Don't snap back at those who say unkind things about you. Instead, pray for God's help for them, for we are to be kind to others, and God will bless us for it'[TLB]."

And I say, "*Amen*, and thank God for all those who bring light to darkness."